Table of Contents

About Summer Learning

Did you know that many children experience learning loss when they do not engage in educational activities during the summer? This means that some of what they have spent time learning over the preceding school year is forgotten during the summer months. However, summer learning loss is something that you can help prevent. Below are a few suggestions for fun and engaging activities that can help children maintain and grow their academic skills during the summer.

- Read with your child every day. Visit your local library together and select books on subjects that interest your child.

- Ask your child's teacher to recommend books for summer reading.

- Explore parks, nature preserves, museums, and cultural centers.

- Look for teachable moments every day. Measuring ingredients for recipes and reviewing maps before a car trip are fun and useful ways to learn or reinforce skills.

- Each day, set goals for your child to accomplish. For example, complete five math problems or read one section or chapter in a book.

- Encourage your child to complete the activities in this book regularly to help bridge the summer learning gap.

About Summer Bridge Activities®

The learning activities in this book are designed to review second grade skills, preview the skills your child will learn in third grade, and help prevent summer learning loss. Your involvement in your child's education is crucial to his or her success. Together with *Summer Bridge Activities*, you can fill the summer months with learning experiences that will deepen and enrich your child's knowledge and prepare him or her for the upcoming school year. Inside this book, you will find the following helpful resources:

Three sections that correspond to the three months of a traditional summer vacation. Each section begins with a goal-setting activity, a word list, and information about the fitness and character development activities located throughout the section.

Learning activity pages. For maximum results, your child should complete two activity pages each day. These engaging, age-appropriate activities cover a range of subjects including reading comprehension, writing, grammar skills, measurement, multiplication, telling time, and more. Each page is numbered by day, and each day includes a space to place a motivational sticker when the activities are complete.

Bonus outdoor learning experiences, science experiments, and social studies exercises. These fun and creative activities are found at the end of each section. Complete the pages with your child throughout each month as time allows.

Flash cards. Help your child cut out these handy cards and use them for practice anytime and anywhere. For children who are entering third grade, use the cards to:

- Sort words under the headings *noun*, *pronoun*, *verb*, *adjective*, or *adverb*.
- Combine prefixes such as *un–*, root words such as *do*, and suffixes such as *–ing* to build new words.

- Build sentences.
- Multiply and divide one-digit numbers.
- Learn fractions.

Certificate of completion. At the end of the summer, fill out the certificate and present it to your child to celebrate learning success!

Stickers. Demonstrate how to place a sticker in the space provided to show that each day's learning activities are complete. Praise your child's effort!

Online companion. Visit *summerlearningactivities.com/sba* with your child to find even more fun and creative ways to prevent summer learning loss.

Skills Matrix

Day	Addition	Algebra	Character Development	Division	Fitness	Fractions	Geometry & Measurement	Grammar	Graphing & Probability	Language Arts	Multiplication	Number Sense	Phonics	Problem Solving	Reading Comprehension	Science	Social Studies	Subtraction	Time & Money	Vocabulary & Spelling	Writing
1							★			★		★									
2		★			★								★						★		
3						★						★			★						
4	★											★	★								
5	★					★						★	★								
6								★				★			★						
7						★		★				★									★
8						★		★					★							★	
9	★							★					★					★		★	
10	★		★															★		★	
11													★	★						★	
12	★							★		★										★	
13									★	★					★						
14	★							★										★			★
15					★						★				★				★		
16						★							★	★							
17	★							★				★			★			★			
18	★																		★	★	★
19												★			★			★			
20	★							★		★								★			★
				★				★		★	BONUS PAGES!				★	★	★			★	★
1	★							★		★										★	
2								★							★			★			
3	★			★				★			★							★			
4					★	★	★	★		★											
5	★							★										★			★
6																			★	★	★
7						★													★	★	
8								★							★					★	
9			★					★			★								★		
10								★	★		★									★	
11								★							★				★		

vi

© Carson-Dellosa

Skills Matrix

Day	Addition	Algebra	Character Development	Division	Fitness	Fractions	Geometry & Measurement	Grammar	Graphing & Probability	Language Arts	Multiplication	Number Sense	Phonics	Problem Solving	Reading Comprehension	Science	Social Studies	Subtraction	Time & Money	Vocabulary & Spelling	Writing
12								★				★							★		★
13					★			★						★	★						
14							★								★						★
15							★	★							★						★
16							★			★										★	
17							★			★					★						
18				★						★					★					★	
19								★		★											★
20							★								★						
BONUS PAGES!							★	★							★	★	★				
1							★	★							★						
2							★													★	★
3	★							★							★			★			
4					★		★			★											
5							★	★		★					★						
6										★	★				★						
7										★	★										
8								★		★					★						★
9				★				★		★					★						
10						★				★	★									★	
11					★					★	★				★						
12						★				★					★						
13			★							★					★						
14						★				★											★
15						★				★					★						
16						★				★									★		
17				★						★											★
18						★			★	★											★
19									★						★						★
20							★	★							★						
BONUS PAGES!	★		★												★	★	★	★			★

Encouraging Summer Reading

Literacy is the single most important skill that your child needs to be successful in school. The following list includes ideas for ways that you can help your child discover the great adventures of reading!

• Establish a time for reading each day. Ask your child about what he or she is reading. Try to relate the material to a summer event or to another book.

• Let your child see you reading for enjoyment. Talk about the great things that you discover when you read.

• Create a summer reading list. Choose books from the reading list (pages ix–x) or head to the library and explore. To choose a book, ask your child to read a page aloud. If he or she does not know more than five words on the page, the book may be too difficult.

• Read newspaper and magazine articles, recipes, menus, maps, and street signs on a daily basis to show your child the importance of reading informational texts.

• Choose a simple book that contains dialogue to read with your child. Read one character's words yourself and have your child read (or act out) another character's words. Speak in a voice that suits your character. Discuss the different points of view the two characters may have.

• Choose a nonfiction book to read or reread with your child. Then, have him or her pretend to be a TV reporter, sharing the "news" of the book you read. Encourage your child to relate details and events from the story in the report.

• Make up stories. This is especially fun to do in the car, on camping trips, or while waiting at the airport. You can also have your child start a story and let other family members build on it.

• Encourage your child to join a summer reading club at the library or a local bookstore.

• Ask your child to compare and contrast different books and stories by the same author. Do they share characters, settings, plots, or themes?

Summer Reading List

The summer reading list includes fiction and nonfiction titles. Experts recommend that second- and third-grade students read for at least 20 minutes each day. Then, ask questions about the story to reinforce comprehension.

Decide on an amount of daily reading time for each month. You may want to write the time on the Monthly Goals page at the beginning of each section in this book.

Fiction

Blume, Judy
The Pain and the Great One

Bunting, Eve
So Far from the Sea

Burns, Marilyn
Spaghetti and Meatballs for All!

Cherry, Lynne
The Great Kapok Tree: A Tale of the Amazon Rain Forest

Cleary, Beverly
Ramona the Pest

Curtis, Gavin
The Bat Boy and His Violin

DeGross, Monalisa
Donovan's Word Jar

dePaola, Tomie
The Art Lesson

Egan, Tim
Dodsworth in Tokyo

Estes, Eleanor
The Hundred Dresses

Falwell, Cathryn
Word Wizard

Henkes, Kevin
The Year of Billy Miller

Holub, Joan
Little Red Writing

Hopkinson, Deborah
Sweet Clara and the Freedom Quilt

Keats, Ezra Jack
Peter's Chair

MacLachlan, Patricia
All the Places to Love

Palatini, Margie
Bedhead
Sweet Tooth

Parish, Peggy
Amelia Bedelia

Pilkey, Dav
Dog Breath

Polacco, Patricia
Mr. Wayne's Masterpiece
Thunder Cake

Rylant, Cynthia
An Angel for Solomon Singer

Say, Allen
Grandfather's Journey

Schotter, Roni
Nothing Ever Happens on 90th Street

Summary Reading List (continued)

Fiction (continued)

Scieszka, Jon
Math Curse
The True Story of the Three Little Pigs

Seuss, Dr.
The Lorax

Silverstein, Shel
A Light in the Attic

Steig, William
Brave Irene

Storad, Conrad J.
Lizards for Lunch: A Roadrunner's Tale

Uchida, Yoshiko
The Bracelet

Van Allsburg, Chris
The Polar Express

Waber, Bernard
Lyle, Lyle, Crocodile

Williams, Margery
The Velveteen Rabbit

Wisniewski, David
The Secret Knowledge of Grown-Ups

Yee, Herbert Wong
A Brand-New Day with Mouse and Mole

Nonfiction

Anno, Masaichiro and Mitsumasa
Anno's Mysterious Multiplying Jar

Berne, Jennifer
On a Beam of Light: A Story of Albert Einstein

Carle, Eric
The Tiny Seed

Christian, Peggy
If You Find a Rock

Dobson, David
Can We Save Them? Endangered Species of North America

George, Jean Craighead
The Tarantula in My Purse and 172 Other Wild Pets

Gibbons, Gail
Nature's Green Umbrella

Hopkinson, Deborah
Annie and Helen

Lester, Helen
Author: A True Story

Locker, Thomas
Water Dance

Martin, Jacqueline Briggs
Farmer Will Allen and the Growing Table

Rosenstock, Barb
Thomas Jefferson Builds a Library

Schwartz, David M.
How Much Is a Million?

Vernick, Audrey
Brothers at Bat: The True Story of an Amazing All-Brother Baseball Team

Monthly Goals

A *goal* is something that you want to accomplish. Sometimes, reaching a goal can be hard work!

Think of three goals to set for yourself this month. For example, you may want to read for 30 minutes each day. Write your goals on the lines and review them with an adult.

Place a sticker next to each goal that you complete. Feel proud that you have met your goals!

1. _____ PLACE STICKER HERE

2. _____ PLACE STICKER HERE

3. _____ PLACE STICKER HERE

Word List

The following words are used in this section. They are good words for you to know. Read each word. Use a dictionary to look up each word that you do not know. Then, write two sentences. Use a word from the word list in each sentence.

coast	glide
crops	history
flexible	shadow
gentle	tame
germs	vapor

1. _____

_____

2. _____

_____

Introduction to Flexibility

This section includes fitness and character development activities that focus on flexibility. These activities are designed to get you moving and thinking about building your physical fitness and your character.

Physical Flexibility

For many people, being flexible means easily doing everyday tasks, such as bending to tie a shoe. Tasks like this can be hard for people who do not stretch often.

Stretching will make your muscles more flexible. It can also improve your balance and coordination.

You probably stretch every day without realizing it. Do you ever reach for a dropped pencil or a box of cereal on the top shelf? If you do, then you are stretching. Try to improve your flexibility this summer. Set a stretching goal. For example, you might stretch every day until you can touch your toes.

Flexibility of Character

It is good to have a flexible body. It is also good to be mentally flexible. This means being open to change.

It can be upsetting when things do not go your way. Can you think of a time when an unexpected event ruined your plans? For example, a family trip to the zoo was canceled because the car had a flat tire.

Unexpected events happen sometimes. How you react to those events often affects the outcome. Arm yourself with the tools to be flexible. Have realistic expectations. Find ways to make the situation better. Look for good things that may have come from the event.

You can be mentally flexible by showing respect to other people. Sharing and taking turns are also ways to be mentally flexible. This character trait gets easier with practice. Over the summer, practice and use your mental flexibility often.

Circle the correct numeral for each number word.

1. forty-five

    54   (45)

2. fifty-eight

    (58)   85

3. eight hundred eighty-one

    (881)   81

4. thirty

    (30)   31

5. three hundred sixty-two

    662   (362)

6. nine hundred twelve

    921   (912)

Write the number word for each numeral.

0: _forty-five_   20: _eight hundred eighty one_   30: _three hundred sixty two_

40: _fifty-eight_   60: _thirty_   80: _nine hundred twelve_

Follow the directions to draw shapes.

7. Draw a shape that has three sides and three angles.

8. Draw a shape with six equal sides and six corners.

9. Draw a shape that has no sides and no corners.

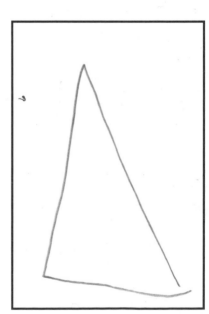

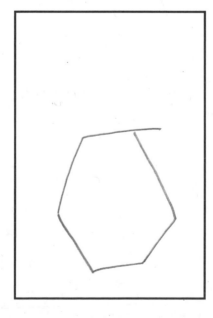

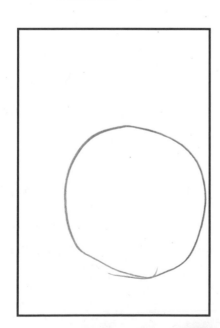

_300_
_100_
_1000_

_+300_
_1_
_301_

DAY 1

Continue each number pattern on the lines. Then, write each rule.

_+100 +100 +100_

300 — 301

10. 300, 400, 500, 600, __700__, __800__, __900__, __1000__

Rule: __add 100__

400
__1__
401

11. 10, 20, 30, 40, __50__, __60__, __70__, __80__, __90__, __100__

Rule: __add 10__

12. 5, 10, 15, 20, __25__, __30__, __35__, __40__, __45__, __50__

Rule: __add 5__

Combine each pair of sentences using the conjunction in parentheses ( ). In each new sentence, place a comma before the conjunction.

EXAMPLE: My grandma raises bees. She has only been stung once. (but)
My grandma raises bees, but she has only been stung once.

13. Avery wanted to bike to the park. He got a flat tire. (but)

Avery wanted to bike to the park, but He got a flatfire

14. Mr. Greene coaches our soccer team. I think he does a great job. (and)

Mr Green coaches our soccer team, and I think he does a great job

15. The fireworks lit up the night sky. Everyone cheered. (so)

The fireworks lit up the night sky, so everyone cheered

16. Tanesha is moving to Illinois. Her family hasn't found a house yet. (but)

Tanesha is moving to Illinois, but Her family hasent found a house yet.

DAY 2

Count the money. Write each amount.

1.
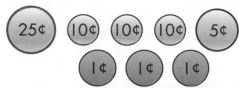

Nikki found a quarter, 3 dimes, a nickel, and 3 pennies under her bed. How much did she find?

 6__ ¢

2.
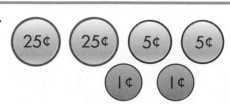

Mai-Lin bought a smoothie. The cashier gave her 3 nickels, a quarter, a dime, and two pennies in change. How much change did she get?

 52 ¢

3.
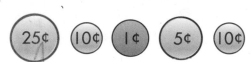

Jacob used 2 quarters, 2 nickels, and 2 pennies to buy some stickers. How much did they cost?

62 ¢

4.

Rita's brother borrowed a quarter, 2 dimes, a nickel, and a penny from her. How much did he borrow?

5__ ¢

Write the number that the symbol represents in each equation.

5. ● + 5 = 11

● = 6

Check: 11 − 5 = 6

6. 5 − ★ = 2

★ = 3

Check: 5 − 2 = 3

7. ▮ + 6 = 14

▮ = 8

Check: 14 − 6 = 8

8. 7 + ▲ = 14

▲ = 7

Check: 14 − 7 = 7

DAY 2

Draw lines to connect syllables to form complete words.

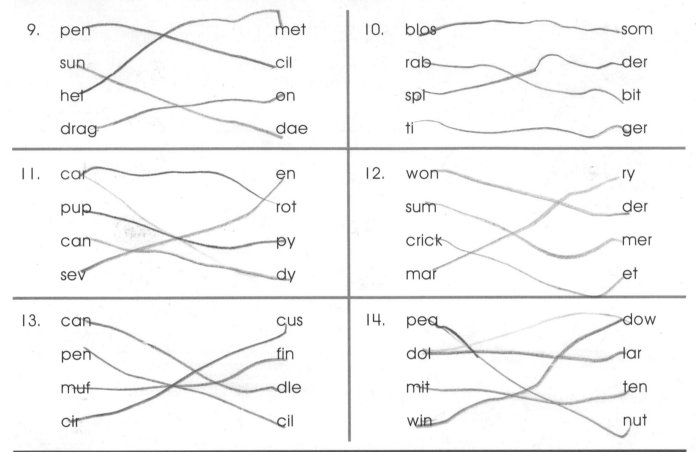

9. pen   met
    sun   cil
    het   on
    drag   dae

10. blos   som
    rab   der
    spl   bit
    ti   ger

11. car   en
    pup   rot
    can   py
    sev   dy

12. won   ry
    sum   der
    crick   mer
    mar   et

13. can   cus
    pen   fin
    muf   dle
    cir   cil

14. pea   dow
    dol   lar
    mit   ten
    win   nut

Stand and Stretch

Test your flexibility with this stretching challenge. Remember to stretch slowly. It takes practice to improve flexibility.

Stand tall and hold a ruler in one hand. Bend slowly at the waist. Reach down until the tip of the ruler touches the ground. Check the ruler to find how close you are to touching the ground. If you can already touch the ground, try to flatten your hands to the floor. Stretch three times. Record your best measurement. Complete this test each week and compare your results.

FITNESS FLASH: Practice a V-sit. Stretch five times.

* See page ii.

6

Write the number that comes before, between, or after each number or numbers.

Before	Between	After
1. _346_ 347	6. 213 _214_ 215	11. 679 _680_
2. _527_ 528	7. 427 _428_ 429	12. 721 _722_
3. _831_ 832	8. 399 _400_ 401	13. 398 _399_
4. _730_ 731	9. 478 _479_ 480	14. 599 _600_
5. _292_ 293	10. 871 _872_ 873	15. 734 _735_

Follow the directions to color equal parts of the shapes.

16. **Color one fourth.**

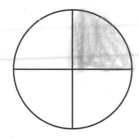

17. **Color two thirds.**

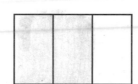

18. **Color four fourths.**

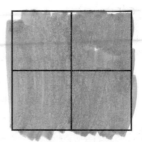

19. **Color one third.**

20. **Color one half.**

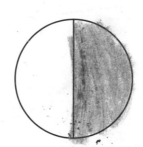

21. **Color three fourths.**

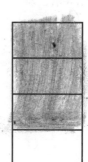

DAY 3

Read the passage. Then, answer the questions.

Helpful Insects and Arachnids

Some insects can destroy crops, such as fruits and vegetables, by eating them. Not all insects are bad, though. Some insects help people. Bees move pollen from flower to flower. This helps flowers make seeds so that there will be more flowers the next year. Bees also produce honey. Ladybugs are helpful insects, too. They eat the insects that chew on plants. Finally, spiders may look scary, but they are helpful. They are not insects. They are arachnids. They catch flies, crickets, and moths in their webs. If you find a spider in your home, ask an adult to help you carefully place it outside. Then, it can do its job.

22. What is the main idea of this passage?

   A.   Insects can destroy crops.

   B.   Ladybugs are beautiful.

   C.   Some insects and arachnids are helpful.

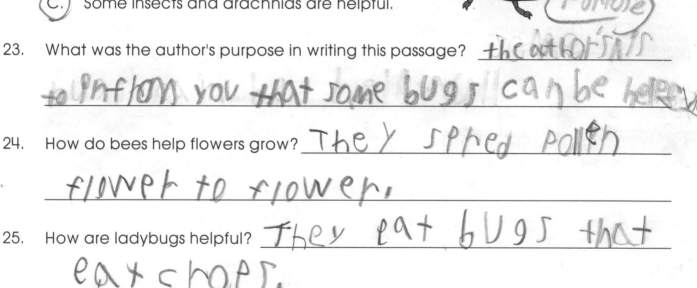

purpose

23. What was the author's purpose in writing this passage? _the author is_
   to inflom you that some bugs can be helpful

24. How do bees help flowers grow? _They spred pollen_
   flower to flower.

25. How are ladybugs helpful? _They eat bugs that_
   eat chops.

26. What are crops? What clues in the passage helped you find the answer? _____
   chops and veges and fruts.
   veggies

Write > (greater than) or < (less than) to compare each pair of numbers.

1. 2 ⟩ 4

2. 64 ⟩ 46

3. 322 ⟩ 100

4. 19 ⟨ 91

5. 29 ⟨ 30

6. 985 ⟩ 850

7. 14 ⟩ 4

8. 124 ⟨ 216

9. 648 ⟨ 846

10. 9 ⟨ 10

11. 592 ⟩ 324

12. 745 ⟨ 746

How many are in each group? Write the number on the line. Then, circle odd or even.

13.
fourteen __14 even__   odd   (even)

14.
nine __odd__   (odd)   even

15.
eighteen __even__   odd   (even)

DAY 4

Add to find each sum.

EXAMPLE:

$\boxed{1}$
32
24
11
+ 19
86

16.
28
14
16
+ 4
6Z

17.
70
26
99
+ 12
207

18.
44
40
2
+ 38
124

19.
57
36
32
+ 89
244

20.
81
12
38
+ 64
195

21.
22
34
9
+ 19
84

22.
67
41
45
+ 15
168

23.
81
28
8
+ 8
125

24.
74
15
33
+ 17
139

Read each word aloud. Listen to the vowel sounds. If the word has a short vowel sound, write _S_ on the line. If the word has a long vowel sound, write _L_ on the line.

EXAMPLE:

just ___S___

25. cape ___L___

26. clock ___S___

27. cute ___L___

28. bug ___S___

29. ship ___S___

30. nice ___L___

31. apple ___S___

32. goat ___L___

33. road ___L___

34. help ___S___

35. read ___L___

FITNESS FLASH: Touch your toes 10 times.

* See page ii.

Find the place value of each underlined digit. Circle the answer.

EXAMPLE:

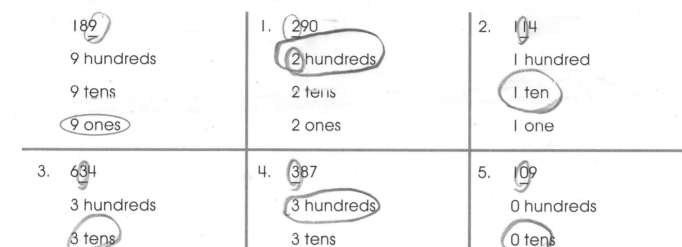

189

9 hundreds

9 tens

(9 ones)

1. (290)

(2 hundreds)

2 tens

2 ones

2. 114

1 hundred

(1 ten)

1 one

3. 634

3 hundreds

(3 tens)

3 ones

4. 387

(3 hundreds)

3 tens

3 ones

5. 109

0 hundreds

(0 tens)

0 ones

6. **Draw lines to divide the circle into four equal parts.**
   What is one part called?

   <u>one forth</u>

7. **Draw a line to divide the triangle into two equal parts.**
   What is one part called?

   <u>one half</u>

8. **Draw lines to divide the rectangle into three equal parts.**
   What is one part called?

   <u>one third</u>

DAY 5

Follow the directions to solve each problem.

9. Start with 15. Write the number that is 10 more. __25__

10. Start with 22. Write the number that is 100 more. __122__

11. Start with 50. Write the number that is 10 more. __60__

12. Start with 335. Write the number that is 100 more. __435__

13. Start with 42. Write the number that is 100 more. __142__

14. Start with 89. Write the number that is 10 more. __99__

Read each word aloud. Then, write _short_ or _long_ for each vowel sound.

15. bug __S__   16. cake __L__

17. cut __S__   18. gum __S__

19. road __L__   20. catch __S__

21. cube __L__   22. clock __S__

23. stick __S__   24. child __L__

25. mop __S__   26. these __L__

27. street __L__   28. log __S__

29. fly __L__   30. boat __L__

CHARACTER CHECK: Think of a book or movie character who shows kindness. How does the character show kindness?

he gave his off a present for vglahtlams bay

1. **Circle the number if 6 is in the hundreds place.**

(629)   486   367

926   (682)   126

(636)   426   (660)

2. **Circle the number if 9 is in the ones place.**

(879)   (429)   (609)

191   (509)   194

(889)   (469)   (209)

3. **Circle the number if 3 is in the tens place.**

(231)   723   (38)

(639)   63   (530)

(333)   (32)   23

4. **Circle the number if 5 is in the tens place.**

(354)   (151)   (555)

185   (250)   (658)

(50)   725   (255)

5. **Circle the number if 4 is in the hundreds place.**

(423)   (484)   124

642   640   432

46   (422)   144

6. **Circle the number if 7 is in the ones place.**

(327)   (147)   (607)

678   478   (447)

799   (997)   (207)

Words that name holidays, places, and products are proper nouns. Underline the proper noun or nouns in each sentence.

7. Have you ever been to Austin, Texas?

8. Let's do a craft for Valentine's Day.

9. My grandmother lives in France.

10. We always buy Papa Pete's pizza when we have family game night.

A+

11. Our neighbors moved here from Nashville, Tennessee.

12. I'd like a glass of orange juice and a bowl of Crunch Os for breakfast.

3+

13. Are you going to wear green on St. Patrick's Day?

Read the passage. Then, answer the questions.

Railroads

Railroads have played an important part in history. For centuries, railroads have helped carry (people) and goods long distances. In the United States, travel was much harder before a railroad connected the eastern and western parts of the country. Workers in the eastern United States built a railroad heading west. A different crew in the west started building a railroad heading east. In 1869, the two lines met in the state of Utah. The crews hammered in a special golden nail to tie the two tracks together. After that, people could travel easily and quickly from one coast of the United States to the other! The next time you stop at a railroad crossing to let a train pass, think about how important railroads have been in history.

14. What is the main idea of this passage?

   A. Railroads played an important part in history.

   B. No one uses railroads today.

   C. You have to stop to let trains go by.

15. What could people (do) once the railroad was completed? People could travel long distanses.

16. Where did the two railroads begin? In the eastern and western of the USA a peaeol hammerd in a specel solder,

17. What did the crews use to join the two tracks? hael to tie the two traks together.

   BEhinus

18. The author states that railroads have played an important part in history. Give

   two reasons from the text that support this point. thay have plaed an thotant

   mant of histor because in the usa pt was wily hard to travel but rea roads

   helped us travel easyer and quiker,

Find six different books. Measure the length of each book to the nearest inch. Write the measurements below. Then, for each book, draw an X above its length on the line plot.

Book 1 _____10_____ inches   Book 4 _____22_____ inches

Book 2 _____7_____ inches   Book 5 _____27_____ inches

Book 3 _____8_____ inches   Book 6 _____8_____ inches

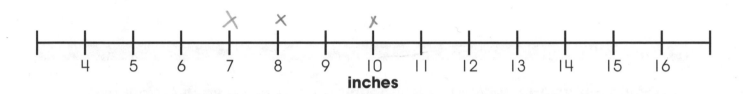

inches

Write each proper noun from the word bank in the correct column.

Memorial Day	Thanksgiving
Russia	Mexico City
Appalachian Mountains	Orchard Plus frozen fruit
Sparkling Bubbles body wash	St. Louis
Clarabelle's pies	Kwanzaa

Holidays   **Products**   **Places**

memorial day   sparkling bubbles (body wash)   Russia

thanksgiving   clarabelle's pies   appalachia mounthi

st.louis   orchard plus frozen fruit   mexica city

          kwanzaa

          st.louis

DAY 7

Write each number in expanded form. Show the number as a sum of hundreds, tens, and ones.

EXAMPLE: 254   200 + 50 + 4

1. 528   _500_ + _20_ + _8_

2. 130   _100_ + _30_ + _0_

3. 689   _600_ + _80_ + _9_

4. 421   _400_ + _20_ + _1_

5. 708   _700_ + _00_ + _8_

6. 567   _500_ + _60_ + _7_

7. 963   _900_ + _60_ + _3_

8. 806   _800_ + _0_ + _6_

Think about your favorite holiday. Describe this holiday using each of your five senses. What do you see, hear, feel, smell, and taste?

my fayerot horday is my berthday. I like Charlit cake to eat. I like the colors of the Decorathons, blue, red and Green. of Dihosaurs. I like to hear every one sing happy birthday to me. I like to feel there a nota full of candy. I like to smell the fresh air of my grand-parihts back yarde.

FITNESS FLASH: Do arm circles for 30 seconds.

* See page ii.

Measure each object below once to the nearest inch and once to the nearest centimeter. Write the measurements on the lines.

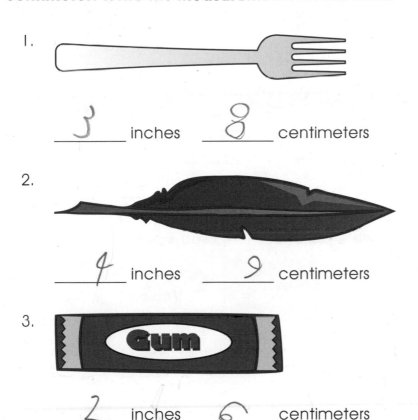

1.

_____3_____ inches   _____8_____ centimeters

2.

_____4_____ inches   _____9_____ centimeters

3.

_____2_____ inches   _____6_____ centimeters

Circle the adverb in each sentence. Then, underline the verb each adverb modifies.

4. The dogs barked loudly at the sound of the doorbell.

5. I looked everywhere for my coat.

6. Nancy swims faster than I do.

7. Greg walked slowly up the driveway.

8. Valerie awoke early on Saturday morning.

9. Let's play outside in the front yard.

DAY 8

When a prefix is added to a base word, it changes the meaning of the word. Circle the prefix in each word. Then, write the letter of the correct definition next to the word.

10. _D_   reopen

11. _B_   unhappy

12. _A_   misplace

13. _E_   unsure

14. _C_   misuse

A. to wrongly place

B. not happy

C. to wrongly use

D. to open again

E. not sure

Look at each word. Write how many vowels you see. Then, read each word aloud. Write how many vowel sounds you hear.

		Vowels	Vowel Sounds				Vowels	Vowel Sounds
15.	puzzle	2	1		23.	radio	3	2
16.	cookies	4	2		24.	carrot	2	2
17.	blocks	1	1		25.	sleep	2	1
18.	alphabet	3	2		26.	wanted	2	2
19.	goat	2	1		27.	heart	2	1
20.	jump	1	1		28.	useful	3	2
21.	pilot	2	2		29.	beautiful	5	4
22.	lion	2	2		30.	water	2	2

FACTOID: Frogs can jump more than 10 times their own body length.

Write the related facts for each fact family.

1.

| 11 |
| 6 5 |

$6 + 5 = 11$

$5 + 6 = 11$

$11 - 5 = 6$

$11 - 6 = 5$

2.

| 4 |
| 5 9 |

$5 + 7 = 9$

$4 + 5 = 9$

$9 - 4 = 8$

$9 - 5 = 4$

3.

| 7 |
| 5 12 |

$7 + 5 = 12$

$5 + 7 = 12$

$12 - 5 = 7$

$12 - 7 = 5$

Draw lines to divide each rectangle into rows and columns. Then, count how many squares are in each rectangle and write the number on the line.

4. 3 rows
    5 columns

    How many squares? _15_

5. 4 rows
    6 columns

    How many squares? _24_

6. 2 rows
    7 columns

    How many squares? _14_
    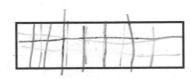

DAY 9

When a suffix is added to a base word, it changes the meaning of the word. Add -*less* or -*ness* to the base word in each sentence.

EXAMPLE:

The children were very ____rest**less**____ today.

7. The ____friendli*ness*____ of the people made us feel at home.

8. Trying to train my dog to roll over is ____hope*less*____.

9. The baby loves the ____soft*ness*____ of her blanket.

10. The ____loud*ness*____ of the noise made me jump.

11. Her ____happi*ness*____ showed on her face.

Read each word in the word bank. If the *y* makes the long *i* sound, as in *fly*, write the word under the fly. If the *y* makes the long *e* sound, as in *baby*, write the word under the baby.

city   dry   eye   happy   sky   story

fly
- dry
- eye
- sky

baby
- city
- happy
- story

 **FITNESS FLASH:** Do 10 shoulder shrugs.

* See page ii.

© Carson-Dellosa

Write the missing sign (+, –, or =) in each number sentence.

1. 6 __+__ 3 = 9 ✓

2. 12 __–__ 6 = 6 ✓

3. 4 __–__ 2 = 2 ✓

4. 4 + 3 __=__ 7 ✓

5. 14 __+__ 1 = 15 ✓

6. 12 __–__ 2 = 10 ✓

7. 9 __=__ 3 – 6 ✓

8. 14 __–__ 4 = 10 ✓

9. 14 – 7 __=__ 7 ✓

10. 4 __–__ 1 = 3 ✓

11. 7 – 3 __=__ 4 ✓

12. 3 __+__ 3 = 6 ✓

13. 8 __+__ 4 = 12 ✓

14. 9 __+__ 2 = 11 ✓

15. 11 __–__ 2 = 9 ✓

Write an addition equation to find the total number of items.
EXAMPLE:

5 + 5 + 5 + 5 = 20

16.

3+3 +3 +3 +3 =15

17.

2 + 2 + 2 + 2 + 2 + 2 + 2 + 2 = 10

18.

7 + 7 + 7 = 21

DAY 10

Underline the compound word in each sentence. Then, draw a line between the two word parts.

EXAMPLE:

Rebecca lives on a house|boat.

19. A raindrop hit the white rabbit on the nose.

20. Let's go visit the lighthouse.

21. Did you hear the doorbell ring?

22. The horses are in the barnyard.

23. I cleaned my bedroom this morning.

24. The snowflakes fell very quickly.

Fairness First

Everyone wants to be treated fairly. Being fair means treating others like you want to be treated. Think about a time when you were treated unfairly. How did that make you feel? Read the following situations. On another sheet of paper, write about what you would do in each situation.

- You have two friends who are staying at your house after your party. It is time for a snack, and you each want a leftover cupcake. Only two cupcakes are left. What would you do? cut ohe cupcake

- Your younger sister is learning to play a new board game. She asks you to play it with her. As you play, you see that she gave you an extra card. The card will help you win. What would you do?

  givit back

CHARACTER CHECK: Help a friend or family member with a task today, such as folding laundry or taking out the trash.

Solve each problem.

1. Allison had 83 marbles. She lost 20 of them. How many marbles does she have left?

63

2. Liam had 66 apples. He gave 42 apples away. How many apples does Liam have left?

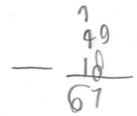
24

3. Shannon walked for 25 minutes. Lori walked for 38 minutes. How many total minutes did the children walk?

4. Nassim saw 18 puppies. Joy saw 49 puppies. How many total puppies did the children see?

49
- 18
67

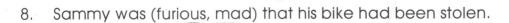

Similar words can have different shades of meaning. Underline the word that best completes each sentence.

5. Levi eagerly (sipped, gulped) the cool water when he came home from his run.

6. The light bulb (shattered, broke) as it hit the floor.

7. "Please don't (gobble, nibble) the cherries so fast!" exclaimed Dad.

8. Sammy was (furious, mad) that his bike had been stolen.

9. Ada (pounded, tapped) on the door, hoping she wouldn't wake the baby.

DAY 11

Read each sentence. Then, write the letter of the underlined word's definition.
EXAMPLE:

____B____ The birds can <u>fly</u>.   A.   a small winged insect

____A____ The spider ate the <u>fly</u>.   B.   to move through the air

10. ___A___ Please turn on the <u>light</u>.   A.   a lamp

     ___B___ The box is <u>light</u>.   B.   not heavy

11. ___B___ <u>Store</u> the books on the shelf.   A.   a place to buy things

     ___A___ I bought a dress at the <u>store</u>.   B.   to put away for the future

12. ___B___ Drop a penny in the <u>well</u>.   A.   healthy

     ___A___ Are you feeling <u>well</u>?   B.   a hole to access underground water

Circle each word that has the /o͞o/ sound, as in _tooth_. Draw an X on each word that has the /o͝o/ sound, as in _hook_.

book   zoo   hoop   wool   cook

hood   soon   pool   scoop   cool

took   stool   food   brook   foot

moon   wood   moose   crook   goose

school   tool   boot   spoon   stood

FACTOID: Manhole covers are round so that they can never fall through.

Draw a line to match the problems that have the same sum.
EXAMPLE:

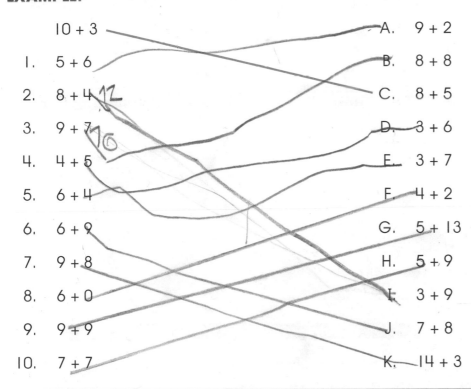

	10 + 3	A.	9 + 2
1.	5 + 6	B.	8 + 8
2.	8 + 4 12	C.	8 + 5
3.	9 + 7 16	D.	3 + 6
4.	4 + 5	E.	3 + 7
5.	6 + 4	F.	4 + 2
6.	6 + 9	G.	5 + 13
7.	9 + 8	H.	5 + 9
8.	6 + 0	I.	3 + 9
9.	9 + 9	J.	7 + 8
10.	7 + 7	K.	14 + 3

Change the spelling of each underlined word to make it plural. Use the word bank if you need help.

feet
geese
knives
leaves
men
mice
teeth

11. more than one <u>man</u> meh

12. more than one <u>tooth</u> teeth

13. more than one <u>leaf</u> leaves

14. more than one <u>goose</u> geese

15. more than one <u>knife</u> knives

16. more than one <u>mouse</u> mice

17. more than one <u>foot</u> feet

DAY 12

Write each word from the word bank under the correct heading.

shirt   pliers   socks   screwdriver   elephant   bear
saw   pants   hammer   fox   deer   hat

Animals	Tools	Clothing
fox	pliers	hat
elephant	hammer	shirt
deer	saw	pants
bear	screwdriver	socks

Collective nouns name groups of people, animals, or things. Choose a collective noun from the box to complete each sentence.

school   swarm   fleet   bouquet   colony

18. Sophie found a ___colony___ of ants under the rock.

19. A ___fleet___ of ships sailed into the harbor.

20. A ___swarm___ of bees flew out of the hive.

21. Vijay picked a ___bouquet___ of flowers for Mom's birthday.

22. Mia saw a ___school___ of fish swim past the canoe.

FITNESS FLASH: Practice a V-sit. Stretch five times.

* See page ii.

vizvs Dog

Study the bar graph. Then, answer each question.

Students' Pets

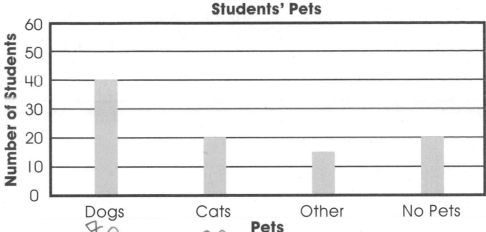

Number of Students

60
50
40
30
20
10
0

Dogs   Cats   Other   No Pets

Pets

70   20

1. How many students have dogs?

40

2. How many more students have dogs than cats?

20

3. Which two categories have the same amount?

cats No Pets

4. How many students have either a cat or a dog?

60

A possessive noun in each sentence is missing an apostrophe. Add an apostrophe like this: Charlotte's kitty.

5. Taylors mask scared her little brother.

6. All of a sudden, the computers screen went blank.

7. Digbys collar is getting too small.

8. Did you see the piñata at Ands birthday party?

9. Moms new sweater looks very cozy.

Read the passage. Then, answer the questions.

Washing Your Hands

Your family and teachers have probably told you many times to wash your hands. You should use warm water and soap. Rub your hands together for as long as it takes to sing the alphabet. Then, sing the song again while you rinse your hands. Soap washes off the **germs**, which are tiny cells that can make you sick. If you do not wash your hands, you can pass a sickness to a friend. Also, you could spread the germs to your eyes or mouth if you touch them before washing your hands. Always remember to wash your hands!

10. What is the main idea of this passage?

    A.   Cells can make you sick.

    B.   Rub your hands together.

    C.   You should wash your hands.

11. How long should you rub your hands together? _Untill you finish singing the abc_

12. What does soap do? _wash away gems._

13. What does the word *germs* mean?

    A.   kinds of soap

    B.   tiny cells that can make you sick

    C.   ways to wash your hands

14. What could happen if you do not wash your hands? _You could get sick and spread gems._

FACTOID: No word in the English language rhymes with *film, gulf,* or *wolf.*

Add and subtract. Regroup when needed.

1. 635
  + 123
  758

2. 987
  − 388
  599

3. 457
  + 394
  851

4. 108
  + 212
  320

5. 852
  − 336
  516

6. 754
  − 288
  466

7. 808
  + 96
  904

8. 552
  − 381
  171

9. 401
  + 599
  1000

10. 1000
  − 999
  0001

Use the number line to help you solve each problem. Mark the number line to show your work.

11. (60) + 35 = 95

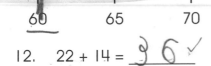

60   65   70   75   80   85   90   95   100

12. 22 + 14 = 36 ✓   36 − 22 = 14

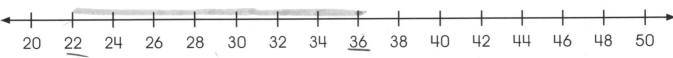

20   22   24   26   28   30   32   34   36   38   40   42   44   46   48   50

13. 100 − 30 = 70

60   70   80   90   100   110

14. 85 − 20 = 65

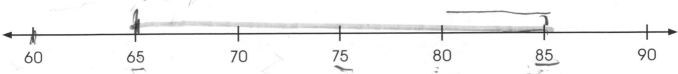

60   65   70   75   80   85   90

DAY 14

Read the sentence pairs. Write an X beside the sentence that happens first.

15. __X__ I planted seeds.

_____ The flowers grew.

16. __X__ Luke started his car.

_____ Luke drove his car.

17. _____ I put on my shoes.

__X__ I put on my socks.

18. __X__ We built a snowman.

_____ Our snowman melted.

19. _____ I brushed my teeth.

__X__ I put toothpaste on my toothbrush.

20. __X__ I climbed into bed.

_____ I fell asleep.

If you had to give away all of the things in your bedroom except for three things, which three things (other than your bed) would you keep? Why?

1 Mr. potatoe head, 2 anqmalstpkes, 3 scareccrow.
1 Id lık to keep mr potato head becaue he ps
1 0 he of my favourıte toys, 2 Id lıke to keep
2 my anqmal stıkers because
2 they are so cute, 3 Id lık to
3 keep my scarecrow because
3 he looks ıke me.

FITNESS FLASH: Touch your toes 10 times.

* See page ii.

Write > (greater than), < (less than), or = (equal to) to compare each expression.

EXAMPLE:

7 + 7 (<) 15

8 + 6 (=) 14

15 (>) 1 + 9

1. 9 + 7 (=) 16

13 − 4 (<) 10

4 + 6 (>) 9

2. 7 + 9 (<) 18

17 − 9 8

14 − 4 (=) 10

3. 8 + 9 (=) 9 + 8

11 − 4 (<) 6 + 2

16 − 4 (<) 3 + 10

4. 5 + 8 (=) 6 + 7

12 − 6 (<) 6 + 6

10 + 1 4 + 7

5. 15 − 5 (>) 13 − 4

18 − 8 (<) 8 + 8

11 + 1 (=) 6 + 6

Underline the root word in each word below. Then, write the definition of the word.

| un– = not | dis– = not, opposite of |
| re– = again | pre– = before |

6. <u>disobey</u> = to not obey

7. <u>reappear</u> = to appear agen

8. <u>unlucky</u> = to not be lucky

9. <u>dishonest</u> = to not be ohest

10. <u>preorder</u> = to order before

11. <u>unsafe</u> = to not be safe

12. <u>rewrite</u> = to rite ageh

13. <u>precook</u> = to cook before

Read the passage. Then, circle the answer that tells what the passage is about.

Birds

All birds are alike in some ways and different in others. They all have wings, but not all of them fly. Some are tame, and some are wild. Some birds sing. Some talk. Some are gentle. Others are not so gentle. Some birds fly very high and far. Others do not. Some birds are colorful while others are plain.

14.   A.   Some birds are tame. Others are not.

      B.   All birds are strange and colorful.

      C.   Birds are alike and different from each other.

Jellyfish Stretch and Glide

It is time to improve your flexibility! Pretend to be a jellyfish with long tentacles. Move around the room. Imagine that you are gliding through the ocean. Stretch your arms from your shoulders to your wrists. Flex each finger. Move your legs smoothly from your hips to your toes. Move your belly, back, and chest from left to right and front to back. Think about how you are moving. You should be slowly stretching several body parts at once. Add soft music or some ocean sounds as you glide toward better flexibility.

> **CHARACTER CHECK:** What do you think is the most important good manner to have?

* See page ii.

Jaeling hi

Solve each problem.

1. Kara had 43 flowers. She sold 9 of them. How many flowers does she have left?

2. Alexander can swim 14 laps in one hour. How many laps can he swim in two hours?

28

3. Michael has 54 toy cars, and Todd has 22 toy cars. How many more cars does Michael have than Todd?

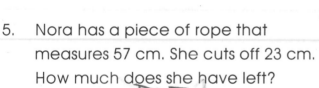

4. Tisha has 19 teddy bears. Brittany has 16 dolls, and Shelby has 8 yo-yos. How many toys do the girls have in all?

5. Nora has a piece of rope that measures 57 cm. She cuts off 23 cm. How much does she have left?

6. Malia is 54 inches tall. Her little sister is 48 inches tall. How much taller is Malia than her sister?

7. A downtown building is 68 meters tall. A nearby building is 85 meters tall. If you stacked the two buildings, how tall would they be?

8. Michael has three cats. One weighs 8 pounds, one weighs 14 pounds, and one weighs 17 pounds. How much do his cats weigh altogether?

39

Read the passage. Then, answer the questions.

The Water Cycle

All water on Earth is part of the same cycle. Water starts out in oceans, lakes, and streams. When the sun heats the water, drops of water rise into the air. Water in this form is called *water vapor*. As the air cools, water droplets form clouds. When the clouds become too heavy with water, they produce rain, sleet, hail, or snow. The water falls back to Earth. Some of the water goes into the soil, where it helps plants grow. Some of the water falls into oceans, lakes, and streams. Then, the water cycle begins again. The next time you drink a glass of water, think about where it came from.

9. What is the main idea of this passage?

   A. All water on Earth moves through a cycle.

   B. Think about where your glass of water came from.

   C. Rain moves water back to Earth.

10. Where does the water cycle begin? _In a lake & ocean_

11. What happens when the sun heats the water? _the water turns into vapor_

12. When do water droplets form clouds? _when the water is to heux for the cloud_

13. What happens when the clouds become too heavy with water? _the water drops_

14. What was the author's purpose for writing this passage? _the life cicle of water_

FACTOID: An ostrich's eye is bigger than its brain.

PLACE STICKER HERE

Add or subtract to solve each problem.

1. 84
   − 42
   42

2. 37
   − 13
   24

3. 69
   + 20
   89

4. 18
   − 4
   14

5. 57
   + 21
   78

6. 28
   − 16
   12

7. 24
   − 11
   13

8. 10
   − 10
   00

9. 23
   + 12
   35

10. 26
   + 22
   48

11. 43
   + 43
   86

12. 91
   + 6
   97

13. 15
   − 9
   6

14. 12
   + 2
   14

15. 49
   − 38
   11

Reflexive pronouns **are special pronouns that end with** *−self* **or** *−selves*. **Circle the reflexive pronoun in each sentence.**

16. I told ⟨myself⟩ that we would have fun, even if it rained.

17. The children were pleased with ⟨themselves⟩ for finding the hidden treasure.

18. George made ⟨himself⟩ a tasty sandwich.

19. The puppy startled ⟨itself⟩ when it looked in the mirror.

20. After working all week, Ms. Hayes gave ⟨herself⟩ the morning off.

21. Did you give ⟨yourself⟩ a haircut?

DAY 17

Read the stories. Decide what will happen next. Then, circle the letter beside the answer.

22. Amy was eating ice cream. Bethany bumped into Amy. What will happen next?

 A. Amy will drink some milk.

 B. Bethany will apologize.

 C. Amy will laugh.

23. Cody was playing tennis with Adam. The sun was very hot. The boys' faces were getting too much sun. What will happen next?

 A. Adam and Cody will go inside.

 B. Cody will walk to the pool.

 C. Cody and Adam will get cold.

Together, the letters _ph_ make the /f/ sound. Read the sentences. Then, write the correct word from the word bank to complete each sentence.

| alphabet | amphibian | elephants | phone |

24. What is your _____phone_____ number?

25. We saw _____elephants_____ at the zoo.

26. Brad wrote the letters of the _____alphabet_____.

27. A frog is an _____amphibian_____.

FITNESS FLASH: Do arm circles for 30 seconds.

* See page ii.

Add to find each sum. Regroup when needed.

1. 324
   + 125
   449

2. 973
   + 24
   997

3. 477
   + 112
   589

4. 206
   + 132
   338

5. 384
   + 88
   472

6. 420
   + 337
   157

7. 688
   + 125
   813

8. 621
   + 126
   747

9. 442
   + 362
   804

10. 175
    + 113
    288

11. 767
    + 104
    871

12. 603
    + 292
    895

13. 398
    + 9
    407

14. 300
    + 500
    800

15. 525
    + 157
    682

Add the prefix *un-* or *re-* to each word. Then, write the meaning of each new word.

16. unsure ____ to not be sure ____

17. Unhappy ____ to not be happy ____

18. Unable ____ to not be able to do somthing ____

19. rewrite ____ to write somthing again ____

20. retell ____ to tell somthing again ____

21. re print ____ to print again ____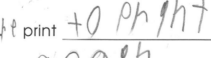

DAY 18

Do you think adults should be allowed to talk on the phone while they are driving? Give your opinion and support it with good reasons.

no because thay can crash
there can if thay do that. or
thay could crash into somwon
else.

Draw hands on each clock to show the correct time.

22.

9:25

23.

5:05

24.

6:35

25.

 one hour later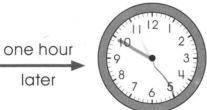

4:50   5 :50

26.

 one hour later

11:10   12 :10

Subtract to find each difference. Regroup when needed.

1. 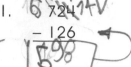 724
   − 126
   Check 598

2. 410
   − 310
   100

3. 7 833
   − 251
   582

4. 978
   − 165
   813

5. 811
   − 704
   107

6. 701
   − 223
   478

7. 583
   − 161
   422

8. 900
   − 140
   760

9. 683
   − 611
   072

10. 896
    − 840
    056

Read the story. Then, answer the questions.

Spilled Milk

A young milkmaid was going to town to sell her cow's milk. It was a long walk. She amused herself by thinking of what she would do with the money she earned. "I'll buy some laying hens from Farmer Brown," she thought. "And then, I'll sell the eggs they lay to the parson's wife. And with the money I make from the eggs, I'll buy a new dress and a hat to match!"

The milkmaid was very pleased with the idea of herself in fancy new clothes. "Won't the other girls be jealous?" she imagined. Thinking of this, she tossed her head and spilled the entire pail of milk.

11. What is the moral of this story?

    A. One good turn deserves another.

    B. Look before you leap.

    C. Don't count your chickens before they hatch.

12. What is the purpose of a fable?

    A. to change the reader's mind about something

    B. to teach a lesson

    C. to give directions

DAY 19

Read the poem. Then, answer the questions.

My Shadow

I have a little shadow that goes in and out with me,

And what can be the use of him is more than I can see.

He is very, very like me from the heels up to the head;

And I see him jump before me, when I jump into my bed.

– Robert Louis Stevenson

13. What does the boy's shadow do when he jumps into bed? _he jums_

too

14. Who does the boy's shadow look like? _the boy._

15. Where does the boy's shadow go? _Where he gaso_

_____

16. Clap as you read the poem. Does it have a steady beat? Why? _yes._

_____

Read each word. Then, circle the letter or letters that are silent.

17. (w)rist

18. thumb

19. (k)nee

20. (k)not

21. (k)night

22. comb

FITNESS FLASH: Do 10 shoulder shrugs.

* See page ii.

Add or subtract to solve each problem. Regroup when needed.

1. 452
    − 132
    389

2. 832
    + 23
    855

3. 153
    + 210
    363

4. 612
    − 224
    398

5. 638
    − 532
    106

6. 34
    + 25
    59

7. 288
    + 13
    301

8. 508
    − 305
    203

9. 374
    + 231
    605

10. 544
    + 234
    778

11. 872
    + 121
    993

12. 688
    + 102
    790

13. 912
    + 87
    999

14. 400
    + 500
    9.00

15. 548
    + 292
    840

Write each verb on the correct ladder.
EXAMPLE:

Present
write
know
laugh
blow
wear
fix
find

blew
blow
find
found
flew
fly
knew

know
laugh
laughed
wear
wore
write
wrote

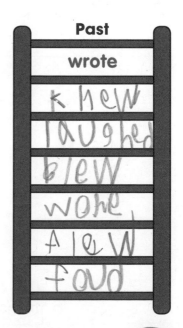

Past
wrote
knew
laughed
blew
wore
flew
found

DAY 20

Read each sentence. Write _R_ if the sentence tells something that is real. Write _F_ if the sentence tells something that is a fantasy.

16. _F_ Jennifer wears a watch on her nose.

17. _R_ A robin flew to the branch in the tree.

18. _R_ Roberto helped his father paint the fence.

19. _F_ Danielle heard two trees talking.

20. _F_ Kyle eats his lunch with a hammer and a saw.

21. _R_ Kayla has two pillows on her bed.

22. _F_ Birds use their beaks to fly.

23. _R_ Derek lost a baby tooth last night.

24. _F_ That cow is driving a bus!

25. _F_ The moose gave the frog a cookie.

Imagine that you are designing a T-shirt for a sports team, a school club, or a special event. Then, draw and color your shirt on another sheet of paper. Write a paragraph about your shirt.

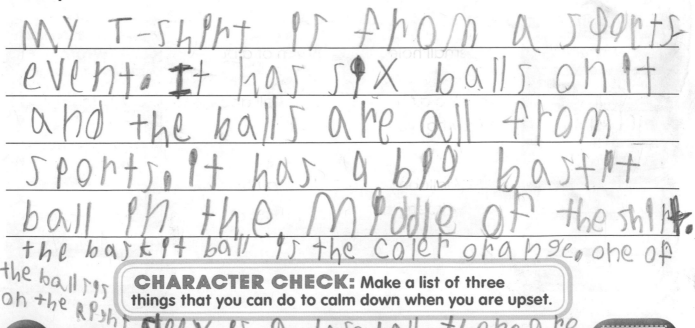

MY T-shirt is from a sports event. It has six balls on it and the balls are all from sports. It has a big bas+it ball in the middle of the shirt. the bas+it ball is the coler orange. one of the balls is on the Rpyht

CHARACTER CHECK: Make a list of three things that you can do to calm down when you are upset.

sleev is a base ball. there are also a amerlc1 han tehis ball and a soccer ball the rest of the sprt is blak.

© Carson-Dellosa

The Impossible Balloon

Can you inflate a balloon in a bottle?

Materials:
- balloon
- plastic bottle (2-liter)

Procedure:
With an adult, put the balloon inside the bottle while holding on to the mouth of the balloon. Stretch the mouth of the balloon over the mouth of the bottle so that it stays in place. Then, put your lips on the bottle. Try to inflate the balloon.

What's This All About?
When you stretch the balloon over the mouth of the bottle, it seals the bottle. No air can get in or out of the bottle. As you try to inflate the balloon, it pushes against the air inside the bottle. The air pushes on the balloon and does not let the balloon get any bigger. Air takes up space and can push things that push it.

More Fun Ideas to Try:
- Try different sizes of bottles to see if you can inflate the balloon in other bottles.
- Try round balloons or long balloons. Before you try the experiment, write what you think might happen.
- Have an adult punch a small hole in the bottom of a bottle. Try the experiment with this bottle.
- Write a letter or an e-mail to a friend or relative. Tell about the experiment you did. Explain how it works and what your results were.

Think About It
- What is the *mouth* of the balloon? What is the *mouth* of the bottle?
- Which section of the experiment tells you what to do, step by step?

* See page ii.

BONUS

Fluid Motion

Will the same object move at different speeds through different fluids?

Speed is the term used to describe how fast an object moves. To calculate speed, divide the distance the object moved by how much time it took to move.

Materials:

- 2 identical jars
- vegetable oil
- stopwatch
- calculator
- water
- two identical marbles
- metric ruler

Procedure:

Fill one jar with water and one jar with vegetable oil.

Hold one marble so that the bottom of the marble touches the top of the vegetable oil. Drop the marble. Use the stopwatch to record the time in seconds that it takes the marble to reach the bottom of the jar. Then, use the ruler to measure the distance the marble traveled. Record your data in the chart.

Follow the same procedure for the second marble and the jar of water. Record your data in the chart.

Divide the distance that each marble traveled by the number of seconds it took for that marble to drop. Use a calculator if you need help.

Measurements			
Fluid	Distance	Time	Speed
vegetable oil			
water			

1. Which marble traveled faster? _____

2. What is the difference between the speed of the first marble and the speed of the second marble? _____

X Marks the Spot

Follow the directions to find the treasure. Draw an X where the treasure is buried. Then, answer the question.

- Start in the Red River Valley.

- Go northeast through Lake Lavender to the Black Forest.

- Go northeast to the Evergreen Forest.

- Travel north to the Purple Mountains.

- Cross the Red River to the Blue Mountains.

- Go south, but do not cross the Red River again.

- The treasure is buried here.

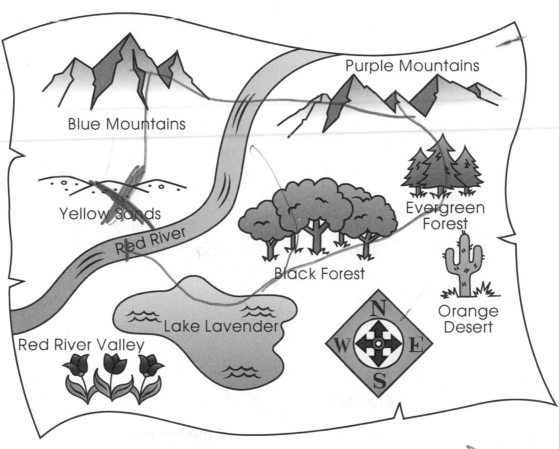

Where is the treasure buried? ___yellow sands___

BONUS

What's the Key?

A map key tells what the symbols on a map stand for. Use the map key to find the objects listed.

1. Circle each city.

2. Draw a square around each baseball park.

3. Draw an X on the state capital.

4. Draw a triangle around the airport.

5. Underline the parks.

6. Draw a star on each university.

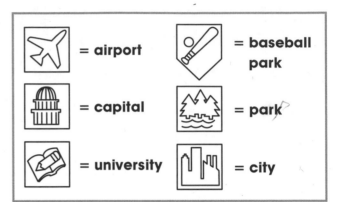

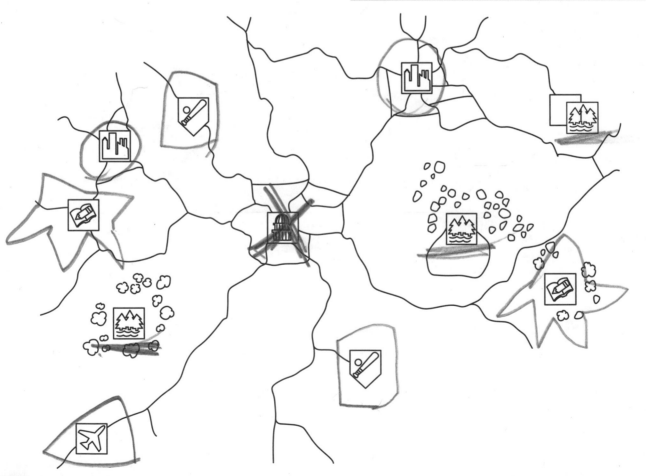

Brent's Street Map

Brent has a street map to help him find his way around his new town. A street map shows where businesses, homes, and other places are located. Look at the street map and answer the questions.

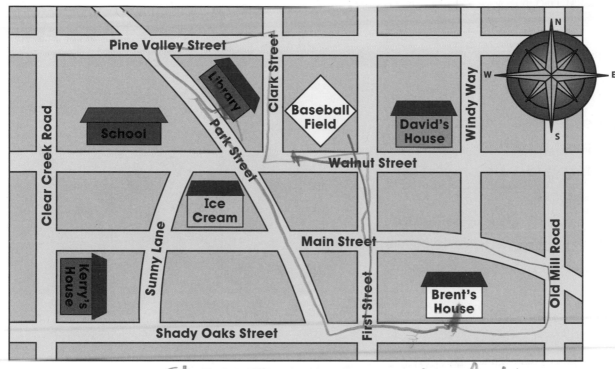

1. Brent lives on _Shady oaks street_.

2. Kerry lives on _clear creak road_.

3. The ice-cream parlor is on _main street_.

4. David lives at the corner of Walnut Street and _Windy way_.

5. The school is on _walnut street_.

6. What two streets could Brent take to get to the library?

   Park street and old mill Road.

BONUS

Take It Outside!

Summer is a great time to read outdoors. Choose a favorite book and find a shady spot to relax and read. Bring a pencil and notebook, too. As you read, write your thoughts, interesting facts, and any new words that you learn. Review your notes at the end of the summer.

Plant a garden! Ask an adult to help you find a large container or choose a spot in the yard. With an adult, go online or visit the library to learn about plants that grow well in your region. Get seeds (vegetable, flower, or herb), some good soil, and water. Plant the seeds. Then, tend your garden by watering and weeding as needed. Record what you planted and when you planted it so that you  can chart the growth of your plants. By the end of summer, you will have a garden to be proud of!

 Head outside with a notebook and pencil. For five minutes, observe what is happening around you. Make a list of the actions you observe, such as a dog barking, a bird flying, a grasshopper jumping, or a person talking. When you are finished, count the number of different verbs on your list. There are so many verbs to observe!

* See page ii.

Monthly Goals

Think of three goals to set for yourself this month. For example, you may want to exercise for 20 minutes each day. Write your goals on the lines and review them with an adult.

Place a sticker next to each goal that you complete. Feel proud that you have met your goals!

1. _____

2. _____

3. _____

Word List

The following words are used in this section. They are good words for you to know. Read each word. Use a dictionary to look up each word that you do not know. Then, write two sentences. Use a word from the word list in each sentence.

advertising	nectar
cabin	popular
illustrated	published
integrity	seasons
molt	tropical

1. _____

_____

2. _____

_____

Introduction to Strength

This section includes fitness and character development activities that focus on strength. These activities are designed to get you moving and thinking about strengthening your body and your character.

Physical Strength

Like flexibility, strength is important for good health. You may think that a strong person is someone who can lift a lot of weight. However, strength is more than the ability to pick up heavy things. Strength is built over time. You are stronger now than you were in preschool. What are some activities that you can do now that you could not do then?

You can gain strength through everyday activities and many fun exercises. Carry grocery bags to build your arms. Ride a bike to strengthen your legs. Swim to strengthen your whole body. Exercises such as push-ups and chin-ups are also great strength builders.

Set goals this summer to improve your strength. Base your goals on activities that you enjoy. Talk about your goals with an adult. As you meet your goals, set new ones. Celebrate your stronger body!

Strength of Character

As you build your physical strength, work on your inner strength, too. Having a strong character means standing up for what you know is right, even if others do not agree.

You can show inner strength in many ways, such as being honest, standing up for someone who needs your help, and putting your best efforts into every task. It is not always easy to show inner strength. Can you think of a time when you used inner strength to handle a situation, such as being teased by another child at the park?

Improve your inner strength over the summer. Think about ways you can show strength of character, such as showing good sportsmanship in your baseball league. Reflect on your positive growth. Be proud of your strong character!

Add to find each sum. Add the numbers in the ones place first and then the numbers in the tens place.

1. 63
    + 48
    111

2. 47
    + 68
    115

3. 19
    + 28
    47

4. 55
    + 59
    114

5. 24
    + 87
    114

6. 64
    + 18
    82

7. 72
    + 48
    120

8. 48
    + 64
    112

9. 37
    + 95
    132

10. 27
    + 56
    83

11. 16
    + 34
    70

12. 33
    + 8
    41

13. 46
    + 78
    124

14. 19
    + 39
    58

15. 28
    + 67
    96

Draw a line to match each present-tense verb with its past-tense form.

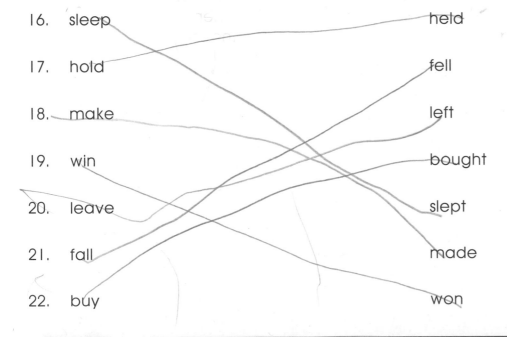

16. sleep   held
17. hold   fell
18. make   left
19. win   bought
20. leave   slept
21. fall   made
22. buy   won

4

DAY 1

Rewrite each set of underlined words as a possessive.

23. The baseball mitt belonging to Chloe is on the dresser. _Chloe's baseball mitt_

24. Have you seen the soccer ball belonging to Jasper? _Jasper's soccer ball_

25. I forgot to bring the goggles belonging to Trinity. _Trinity's goggles_

26. The golf clubs belonging to Grandpa are in the basement. _Grampa's Golf clubs_

27. The ballet shoes belonging to Cassidy are too small. _Cassidy's ballet shoes_

28. Halley left the tennis racquet belonging to Ian on the bus. _Ian's tennis racquet_

Read the sentences. Look at each underlined word. Then, color in the circle to tell if the word is spelled correctly or incorrectly.

		CORRECT	INCORRECT
EXAMPLE:	We <u>ate</u> toast with jam on it.	●	○
29.	We <u>wint</u> to the store for some bread and milk.	○	●
30.	The dog will hunt for his <u>boone</u>.	○	●
31.	We will <u>plant</u> our garden.	●	○
32.	The <u>keng</u> asked the queen to dance.	○	●
33.	<u>Think</u> of a good name for a cat.	●	○

FACTOID: Birds could never be astronauts. They need gravity in order to swallow!

Subtract to find each difference. Subtract the numbers in the ones place first and then the numbers in the tens place.

```
    5 1
  - 3 8
    13
```

1.
```
  6  7̶5̶ ↑5
    - 2 6
      4 9
```

2.
```
  7  8̶2̶ 12
    - 3 7
      4 5
```

3.
```
  ^  2̶7̶ ↑7
    - 1 9
      0 8
```

4.
```
  5  6̶5̶ 15
    -   9
      5 6
```

5.
```
  7  8̶3̶ 13
    - 2 4
      5 9
```

6.
```
  8  9̶5̶ 15
    - 7 8
      1 7
```

7.
```
  4  5̶6̶ 16   16.
    - 1 7       - 7
      3 9        4
```

8.
```
  7  8̶1̶ 11
    -   6
      7 5
```

9.
```
  4  5̶4̶ 14
    - 3 9
      1 5
```

10.
```
  5  6̶4̶ 14
    - 1 8
      4 6

      6
```

11.
```
  2  3̶5̶ 15
    - 1 6
      1 9
```

Write the past-tense form of each verb to complete each sentence.

12. Chang _____made_____ a card for Alfonso.
     (make)

13. Lindsey _____took_____ her cat to the vet.
     (take)

14. She _____bought_____ enough bread for a week.
     (buy)

15. Claire and I _____saw_____ the movie last night.
     (see)

16. I _____ to the gas station.
     (go)

17. The bird _____flew_____ to the nest.
     (fly)

© Carson-Dellosa

DAY 2

Read the poem. Then, answer the questions.

Sing a Song of Summer

Sing a song of summer
with arms stretched open wide.
Run in the sunshine.
Play all day outside.

Hold on to the summer
as long as you may.
Autumn will come quickly
and shorten the day.

Play in the water.
Roll in the grass.
It won't be long now
before you'll be in class.

18. Which sentence tells the main idea of the poem?

    A.   Enjoy summer while it lasts.   B.   Summer gets too hot.

    C.   School starts in the autumn.   D.   It is fun to sing songs.

19. What season comes after summer?

    A.   winter   B.   spring

    C.   autumn   D.   October

20. Write an X beside each thing you can do in the summer.

    _____ play outside   _____ rake leaves

    _____ go swimming   _____ build a snowman

FITNESS FLASH: Do five push-ups.

* See page ii.

PLACE STICKER HERE

Add or subtract to solve each problem.

1.	433 + 18	2.	762 − 28	3.	819 + 20	4.	453 − 5	5.	658 + 24

6.	544 − 18	7.	234 − 9	8.	372 + 9	9.	675 − 47	10.	981 + 11

Write *am*, *is*, or *are* to complete each sentence.

11. I _____ the tallest girl on the team.

12. My lunch _____ in my backpack.

13. We _____ in line for the roller coaster.

14. I _____ ready to go swimming.

15. Jonah's friends _____ laughing at a joke.

16. Aunt Ebony _____ listening to music.

17. We _____ painting the room blue.

CHARACTER CHECK: Brainstorm a list of ways that you can show responsibility. Post your list somewhere that you will see it often.

DAY 3

Write a multiplication equation to show the number of items in each group.
EXAMPLE:

$$3 \times 4 = 12$$

18.

_____

19.

_____

20.

_____

Monkeying Around

With an adult, visit a playground. Find the monkey bars. Begin by swinging by your arms from bar to bar. If you need practice, set a goal such as swing across, rest, and go back. If you are very good at swinging across the bars, see how many times you can go back and forth. You are not just monkeying around! You are improving your upper body strength!

FACTOID: Grown-ups blink about 10 times a minute, but babies blink only once or twice a minute.

* See page ii.

PLACE STICKER HERE

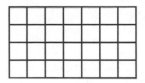

DAY 4

Find the area of each figure.

1.

$$\underline{\hspace{3cm}} \times \underline{\hspace{3cm}} = \underline{\hspace{3cm}}$$
base   height   total area

2.

$$\underline{\hspace{3cm}} \times \underline{\hspace{3cm}} = \underline{\hspace{3cm}}$$
base   height   total area

3.

$$\underline{\hspace{3cm}} \times \underline{\hspace{3cm}} = \underline{\hspace{3cm}}$$
base   height   total area

4.

$$\underline{\hspace{3cm}} \times \underline{\hspace{3cm}} = \underline{\hspace{3cm}}$$
base   height   total area

Look at each underlined word. On the line, write whether it is a *noun*, *pronoun*, *verb*, *adjective*, or *adverb*.

5. _____ The old green <u>tent</u> smelled of leaves and woodsy air.

6. _____ Dad <u>quickly</u> unzipped the tent's windows.

7. _____ The smell of <u>crispy</u> bacon filled the air.

8. _____ A cool stream <u>ran</u> along one side of the campsite.

9. _____ <u>I</u> couldn't wait to start the campfire.

10. _____ We <u>roasted</u> six ears of corn.

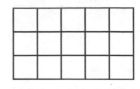

DAY 4

Mark each fraction on the number line.

11. $\frac{3}{4}$

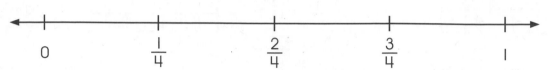

$0 \qquad \frac{1}{4} \qquad \frac{2}{4} \qquad \frac{3}{4} \qquad 1$

12. $\frac{5}{8}$

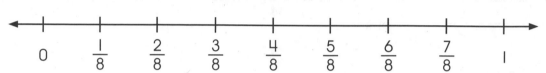

$0 \quad \frac{1}{8} \quad \frac{2}{8} \quad \frac{3}{8} \quad \frac{4}{8} \quad \frac{5}{8} \quad \frac{6}{8} \quad \frac{7}{8} \quad 1$

13. $\frac{1}{3}$

$0 \qquad \frac{1}{3} \qquad \frac{2}{3} \qquad 1$

14. $\frac{10}{10}$ or I whole

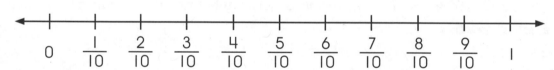

$0 \quad \frac{1}{10} \quad \frac{2}{10} \quad \frac{3}{10} \quad \frac{4}{10} \quad \frac{5}{10} \quad \frac{6}{10} \quad \frac{7}{10} \quad \frac{8}{10} \quad \frac{9}{10} \quad 1$

Add the missing commas to each address below. Use this symbol to add them: ⌃ .

81 Riverwood Rd.
Charlotte NC 28870

132 West Billingsley Lane
Taos NM 87571

1425 Newtown Terrace #12
Providence RI 02906

21896 Langston Blvd.
San Diego, CA 92119

FITNESS FLASH: Do 10 lunges.

* See page ii.

PLACE STICKER HERE

Use a red pencil to check the problems. Write a √ beside each correct answer. Write an X beside each incorrect answer.

1.	423 + 138 561	2.	784 − 107 618	3.	434 + 128 562	4.	324 + 267 592	5.	38 + 19 57

6.	667 − 419 247	7.	410 − 125 305	8.	948 − 819 129	9.	546 − 317 218	10.	634 − 571 63

11.	342 − 237 105	12.	467 + 161 628	13.	861 − 671 210	14.	933 − 673 260	15.	429 + 364 893

Write *has* or *have* to complete each sentence.

16. We _____ fun plans for this summer.

17. My mom _____ Friday off.

18. My dad _____ a new book.

19. The girl _____ a hat.

20. Lia and I _____fruit in our lunches.

21. The doghouses _____new roofs.

22. His sister _____ dance shoes.

23. The club _____many members.

Read the passage. Then, answer the questions.

Mercer Mayer

Mercer Mayer's books can be found in many libraries and bookstores. He has both written and illustrated books. Some of his most popular books include *There's a Nightmare in My Closet*; *Liza Lou and the Yeller Belly Swamp*; *Just for You*; and *A Boy, a Dog, and a Frog*. He likes to write about things that happened to him as a child.

Mercer Mayer was born on December 30, 1943, in Arkansas. When he was 13, he moved to Hawaii with his family. After high school, he studied art. Then, he worked for an advertising company in New York. He published his first book in 1967. He and his wife work together on the Little Critter stories. Now, he works from his home in Connecticut.

24. This passage is called a *biography*. Based on what you read, what do you think a biography is?

    A. a made-up story about a character from a book

    B. a true story that tells about the life of a real person

    C. a short, funny story

Write *T* for statements that are true. Write *F* for statements that are false.

25. _____ Mercer Mayer is a character in a book.

26. _____ Mercer Mayer writes about things that happened to him as a child.

27. _____ Mercer Mayer lived in many different places.

28. _____ Mercer Mayer never worked in New York.

29. Go to the library, or go online with an adult. Do some research on another children's author. Write a paragraph about the author you chose on a separate sheet of paper. How is the author similar to Mercer Mayer? How is he or she different?

Write the time shown on each clock.

1.

____:____

2.

____:____

3.

____:____

4.

____:____

5.

____:____

6.

____:____

Use the prefix and suffix meanings in the box to help you write a definition for each word.

un–/non– = not	–er/–or = one who
re– = again	–tion = act or process of
dis– = not, opposite of	–ness = state or condition of

7. gardener = _____

8. dishonest = _____

9. addition = _____

10. nonfiction = _____

11. unhealthy = _____

12. illness = _____

13. collector = _____

14. reuse = _____

Circle the root word in each word below. Then, think of another word that has the same root. Write the new word on the line.

15. unreasonable _____

16. disinterested _____

17. misbehaving _____

18. unbelievable _____

19. bicycling _____

20. telephone _____

Which character from a book that you have read is most like you? How are you and this character alike?

_____

_____

_____

_____

_____

_____

_____

FACTOID: Koala fingerprints look similar to human fingerprints.

PLACE STICKER HERE

Draw hands on each clock to show the correct time.

1.

12:45

2.

9:17

3.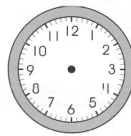

12:31

4.

8:28

5.

5:40

6.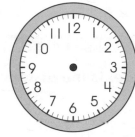

12:09

Add the suffixes -ed and -ing to each base word. You may need to drop letters from or add letters to some words before adding the suffixes.

7. rake

8. jump

9. hug

10. cook

11. skate

_____

_____

12. wrap

13. sneeze

14. pop

15. talk

16. smile

_____

_____

DAY 7

Write the letter of the correct definition next to each word.

17. _____ cheerful

18. _____ sleepless

19. _____ colorful

20. _____ sunless

21. _____ helpful

A. ready to help

B. without sun

C. very cheery

D. having many colors

E. not able to sleep

Perimeter is the distance all the way around a shape. Write the perimeter of each figure.

22.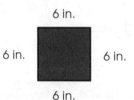
6 in.
6 in.   6 in.
6 in.

perimeter = _____ in.

23.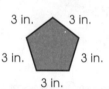
3 in.   3 in.
3 in.   3 in.
3 in.

perimeter = _____ in.

24.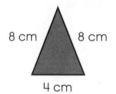
8 cm   8 cm
4 cm

perimeter = _____ cm

25.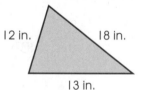
12 in.   18 in.
13 in.

perimeter = _____ in.

26.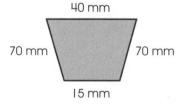
40 mm
70 mm   70 mm
15 mm

perimeter = _____ mm

27.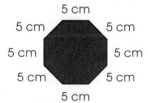
5 cm
5 cm   5 cm
5 cm   5 cm
5 cm   5 cm
5 cm

perimeter = _____ cm

PLACE STICKER HERE

Solve the word problems about time.

1. Caleb got on the bus at 7:30. It took him 20 minutes to get to school. What time did he arrive?

   _____

2. Aliya's piano lesson started at 4:15. It lasted half an hour. What time did she finish her lesson?

   _____

3. It started raining at 6:05. It rained for 45 minutes. What time did it stop raining?

   _____

4. Mr. Domingo's class got to the museum at 9:00. They left two and one-half hours later. What time did they leave?

   _____

Write the word *went* or *gone* to complete each sentence. Remember: The word *gone* needs another word to help it, such as *has* or *have*.

5. Ben _____ home after school.

6. Jessi has _____ shopping for a new coat.

7. Deanna _____ with Andrew to play.

8. We will be _____ on vacation all week.

9. My mother _____ to work this morning.

DAY 8

Read the passage. Then, answer the questions.

Nightly Navigators

Bats help people in many ways. Most bats eat insects at night. This helps to keep the number of insects low. Bats eat mosquitoes, mayflies, and moths. Bats also pollinate and spread the seeds of many tropical trees.

Bats are the only flying mammals on Earth. There are more than 900 kinds of bats. Some bats are only 1.3 inches (3.3 centimeters) long. Some are more than 16 inches (40 centimeters) long. Most bats eat only insects. Some bats eat fruit and the nectar of flowers.

10. How many different kinds of bats are there?

    _____

11. What do bats eat? _____

12. How large can some types of bats grow? _____

13. What is the main idea of the first paragraph? _____

14. What evidence does the author give to support the main idea in the first

    paragraph? _____

    _____

15. Name three types of insects that bats eat. _____

    _____

FACTOID: Your heart is about the same size as your fist.

PLACE STICKER HERE

Circle the coins to equal each amount shown.

1. 34¢ (10¢) (10¢) (5¢) (5¢) (1¢) (1¢) (1¢) (1¢) (1¢)

2. 72¢ (10¢) (10¢) (10¢) (10¢) (10¢) (10¢) (10¢) (1¢) (1¢)

3. 25¢ (5¢) (5¢) (5¢) (5¢) (5¢) (5¢) (1¢) (1¢)

4. 49¢ (10¢) (10¢) (10¢) (10¢) (5¢) (1¢) (1¢) (1¢) (1¢)

Write a word from each box to complete each sentence.

5. The train will _____.

   The train is _____.

   The train has _____.

   | stop |
   | stopped |
   | stopping |

6. The baby can _____.

   The baby is _____.

   The baby _____.

   | clap |
   | clapped |
   | clapping |

7. The rabbit is _____.

   The rabbit _____.

   The rabbit can _____.

   | hop |
   | hopped |
   | hopping |

DAY 9

Round each number to the nearest ten.

8. 56 _____

9. 142 _____

10. 33 _____

11. 289 _____

12. 11 _____

Round each number to the nearest hundred.

13. 342 _____

14. 586 _____

15. 204 _____

16. 650 _____

17. 817 _____

A Sticky Situation

Having *integrity* means showing what you believe through your actions. Read the following situation. On a separate sheet of paper, write about what you would do.

Situation: You know that it is important to be honest. One day when you are playing at your best friend's house, she accidentally breaks her mom's cookie jar. She glues the pieces together and places it back on a table. Later in the day, her mom finds you two playing and questions both of you about the cookie jar. What would you do?

FITNESS FLASH: Do 10 squats.

* See page ii.

PLACE STICKER HERE

Mr. Cohen manages a bakery. He is tracking how many loaves of bread the bakery has sold each month so far this year. Fill in the pictograph below based on the following data.

January = 40 loaves
February = 40 loaves
March = 60 loaves
April = 80 loaves
May = 85 loaves
June = 95 loaves

Month	Loaves of Bread Sold
Jan.	
Feb.	
March	
April	
May	
June	

Key
⌓ = 10 loaves

Cross out each incorrectly used or misspelled word in the journal entry. Write the correct word above it.

September 14, 2015

Yesterday, we learn about colors in art. We make a color wheel. We found out that

there is three basic colors. They am called *primary colors*. Red, yellow, and blue

are primary colors. Primary colors mix to make other colors. Red and yellow makes

orange. Yellow and blue make green. Blue and red make purple. Orange, green,

and purple is secondary colors.

DAY 10

Circle the meaning of each underlined word.

1. She has on a <u>dark</u> purple dress.

    A. night   B. not light

2. We were <u>safe</u> on the rock.

    A. without danger   B. place to keep things

3. Fernando had to be home before <u>dark</u>.

    A. morning   B. night

4. I took a <u>trip</u> to the museum.

    A. a visit   B. to stumble

5. The <u>bank</u> closes at five o'clock.

    A. place where money is kept   B. a steep hill

Solve each problem.

6. 20 x 9	7. 50 x 7	8. 90 x 4	9. 80 x 3	10. 40 x 6
11. 30 x 9	12. 60 x 8	13. 10 x 8	14. 20 x 3	15. 70 x 1

CHARACTER CHECK: Look up *unique* in a dictionary. How are you unique?

PLACE
STICKER
HERE

Count the groups of money in each problem. Draw an X on the group that is worth more.

1.

2.

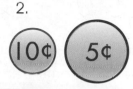 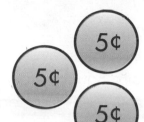

3.

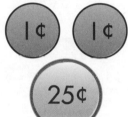 

4.

Adjectives describe nouns. Some adjectives describe how things look or sound. Some adjectives describe how things feel or taste. Write the best adjective from the word bank to complete each sentence.

| rainy | equal | low | tiny |

5. I put an _____ amount of soup in my bowl and yours.

6. There is a _____ bug on the leaf.

7. Latoya stepped over the _____ wall.

8. She saw a rainbow in the sky on the _____ day.

DAY II

Read the passage. Then, answer the questions.

Continents

Earth has seven continents: Africa, Antarctica, Asia, Australia, Europe, North America, and South America. These continents were once a large piece of land. The land split millions of years ago. Large pieces of land drifted apart. The oceans filled the spaces between the pieces of land. The continents we know today are the result. Each continent looks different and has different plants, animals, and weather. North America does not have tigers, but Asia does. Antarctica does not have a jungle, but South America does. The continents are similar in some ways. Some similarities may be because the continents were once one large piece of land.

9. What is the main idea of this passage?

    A. Earth is made of land and water.

    B. Earth has seven continents that were once one piece of land.

    C. Earth has many types of animals, plants, and weather.

10. List the seven continents. _____

    _____

11. When did the continents form?_____

12. What type of land can you find in South America? _____

13. Why might continents with an ocean between them have similarities?

    _____

    _____

FACTOID: Hummingbirds are the only birds that can hover and fly upside down.

© Carson-Dellosa

Make one dollar in change five different ways.
EXAMPLE:

quarters	**2**	1.	quarters	_____	2.	quarters	_____
dimes	**4**		dimes	_____		dimes	_____
nickels	**2**		nickels	_____		nickels	_____
pennies	**0**		pennies	_____		pennies	_____
total	$ **1.00**		total	$ _____		total	$ _____

3.	quarters	_____	4.	quarters	_____	5.	quarters	_____
	dimes	_____		dimes	_____		dimes	_____
	nickels	_____		nickels	_____		nickels	_____
	pennies	_____		pennies	_____		pennies	_____
	total	$ _____		total	$ _____		total	$ _____

Circle the adjectives in each sentence.
EXAMPLE:

The (big) (red) wagon rolled down the hill.

6. Justin likes a soft pillow.

7. The hikers climbed a steep hill.

8. The door made a screechy noise.

9. The hot, wet sand felt good on our feet.

DAY 12

Round each number to the nearest ten and nearest hundred. Then, write each number in expanded form.

	Ten	Hundred	Expanded Form
EXAMPLE: 256	**260**	**300**	**200 + 50 + 6**
10. 542			
11. 311			
12. 898			
13. 426			
14. 657			
15. 102			

Write about something that you could reuse or recycle. How would you reuse or recycle it?

_____

_____

_____

_____

_____

_____

FITNESS FLASH: Do five push-ups.

* See page ii.

PLACE STICKER HERE

It takes two steps to find the solution to each problem below. Write both equations you use to find each solution.

EXAMPLE:

Ezra has $20. He buys 3 fossils for $3 each. How much money does he have left?

$$3 \times 3 - 9 \qquad 20 - 9 = 11$$

1. Zoe had a garden party with 6 friends. Each friend got 2 packets of flower seeds to take home. Zoe kept 4 packets of seeds for her own garden. How many packets of flower seeds were there in all?

    _____   _____

2. Azim had 55 grapes. He fed his 8 chickens 6 grapes each. How many grapes were left?

    _____   _____

3. Kendall's mom makes picnic blankets. She can make 9 blankets with 27 yards of fabric. How much fabric would she need to make 12 blankets?

    _____   _____

Circle the adjectives that describe each underlined noun.

4. I have a blue and purple <u>coat</u>.

5. The little green <u>snake</u> climbed the tree.

6. Tasha made a dress from colorful, soft <u>cloth</u>.

7. The dark gray <u>cloud</u> is over my house.

8. I wore my new brown <u>sandals</u> today.

DAY 13

Read the story. Then, number the events in the order that they happened.

Snowed In

It snowed for three days. When it stopped, the snow was so deep that Ivan and Jacob could not open the cabin door. The men climbed through the upstairs window to get outside. They spent hours shoveling the snow away from the door. At last, they could open the door.

9. _____ The men climbed out the window.

10. _____ It snowed for three days.

11. _____ Ivan and Jacob opened the door.

12. _____ The men shoveled snow for hours.

Quick-Crawling Crab

Have you ever seen a crab crawling on the beach? If you try to move like those fast crustaceans, you can build your upper body, lower body, and core strength.

Sit on the floor. Place your hands behind you and feet in front of you flat on the ground. Use your arms and legs to lift your body off of the ground. Now, crab-walk backward a few yards. Then, crab-walk forward. It is hard to keep your weight off the ground for long!

Once you have mastered the crab-walk, you can make the activity more challenging. Use a stopwatch or timer to see how long you can crab-walk, or increase your speed. Practice the crab-walk throughout the summer, and you will feel your body become stronger.

FACTOID: The Bahamas once had an undersea post office.

* See page ii.

PLACE STICKER HERE

Find the length of each line segment in inches. Round each number to the nearest inch. Write the measurements in the boxes. Then, add the measurements.

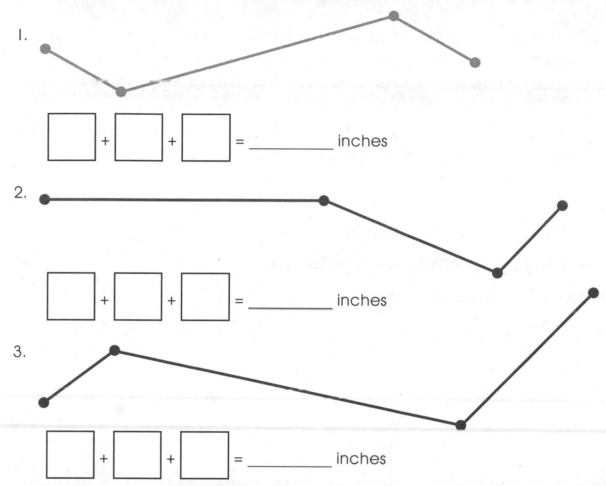

1.

☐ + ☐ + ☐ = _____ inches

2.

☐ + ☐ + ☐ = _____ inches

3.

☐ + ☐ + ☐ = _____ inches

Write a story about a character who does something for the first time. Maybe the person is starting a new school or joining a soccer team. If you need more space, use a separate sheet of paper.

_____

_____

_____

_____

Read the passage. Then, answer the questions.

Sleep

Are you ever sleepy in the middle of the day? Children need about 8 to 11 hours of sleep each night. During sleep, your body rests and gets ready for another day. It is important to be rested for school every morning. If you are tired, you might have trouble paying attention to your teacher. If you have a hard time falling asleep, try reading a book instead of watching TV before bedtime. Go to bed at the same time every night. Play soft music to help you get sleepy. Soon, you will be dreaming!

4.   What is the main idea of this passage?

    A.   Getting enough sleep is important.

    B.   Reading a book can help you go to sleep.

    C.   You should dream every night.

5.   How much sleep do children need?_____

6.   What might happen at school if you are tired?_____

_____

7.   What can you do instead of watching TV at bedtime? _____

_____

8.   When should you go to bed?

    A.   10 P.M.

    B.   only when you feel sleepy

    C.   at the same time every night

 **FITNESS FLASH:** Do 10 lunges.

* See page ii.

 PLACE STICKER HERE

Measure the length of each object in centimeters.

1.  _____ cm

2. _____ cm

3.  _____ cm

4.  _____ cm

5. _____ cm

6.  _____ cm

Write an adjective to complete each sentence.

7. Gabriel showed me the _____ picture.

8. The _____ puppy is chasing his tail.

9. That _____ bird flies south for the winter.

10. Stephen carried the _____ suitcase.

11. That book with the _____ cover is mine.

Circle the letter next to the main idea of each paragraph.

12. Sometimes, I have strange dreams. Once, I dreamed I was floating inside a spaceship. When I woke up, I thought I was still floating. I reminded myself that it was just a dream. When I told my mom about it, she said that she sometimes has strange dreams, too.

    A.   I dreamed I was floating in space.

    B.   My mom had the same dream I did.

    C.   Sometimes, we have strange dreams.

13. I like to read. In the summer, I go to the library twice a week. I check out books about lemurs and airplanes. I also like to read about rain forests. The librarian helps me find books I will like.

    A.   I read books about race cars in the summer.

    B.   I find books to read at the library.

    C.   Librarians are friendly and helpful.

Write a short story about a character who is honest. Give your story a happy ending. Then, share your story with a family member.

_____

_____

_____

_____

_____

_____

PLACE
STICKER
HERE

One meter is 100 centimeters. Circle your estimate for each question.

EXAMPLE:

A dictionary is

A.   taller than one meter.

B.   shorter than one meter.

1.   A house is

A.   taller than one meter.

B.   shorter than one meter.

2.   A baby is

A.   longer than one meter.

B.   shorter than one meter.

3.   Your front door is

A.   taller than one meter.

B.   shorter than one meter.

4.   A pencil is

A.   longer than one meter.

B.   shorter than one meter.

5.   A paper clip is

A.   longer than one meter.

B.   shorter than one meter.

Write the two words that make each contraction.
EXAMPLE:

hasn't _____**has not**_____

6.   I'm _____

7.   you'll _____

8.   wouldn't _____

9.   we've _____

10.   we'd _____

11.   you're _____

12.   she's _____

13.   isn't _____

14.   I'll _____

DAY 16

Use the table of contents to answer the questions.

15. On which page should you begin reading about where ants live?

_____

16. Which chapter would tell about the different kinds of ants?

_____

17. On which page would you look to find the index?

_____

18. What is the title of the first chapter?

_____

Table of Contents

Draw an X over each misspelled word. Write each word correctly.

19. Marcus has a new electrik car.   _____

20. Bonnie takes the fast trane to work.   _____

21. Let's keap together when we go.   _____

22. My dad drives a large dump truk.   _____

23. Let's plae baseball.   _____

FACTOID: Old beds were held up with rope. That's why we say, "Sleep tight."

PLACE STICKER HERE

Estimate the volume of each item. Circle your answer.

1.

A.   100 liters

B.   10 liters

C.   1 liter

2.

A.   100 milliliters

B.   1 milliliter

C.   1 liter

3.

A.   1 liter

B.   150 liters

C.   15 milliliters

4.

A.   5 milliliters

B.   50 milliliters

C.   500 milliliters

Write the two words that make each contraction.

5.   she's _____

6.   he's _____

7.   aren't _____

8.   you've _____

9.   I've _____

10.   I'd _____

11.   it's _____

12.   haven't _____

13.   she'll _____

14.   shouldn't _____

15.   we'll _____

16.   we're _____

DAY 17

Read the passage. Then, answer the questions.

Changing with the Seasons

We change the types of clothes we wear with the seasons to protect us from the weather. Animals do the same when the seasons change.

For example, the arctic fox has a thick, white fur coat in the winter. A white coat is not easy to see in the snow. This helps the fox hide. When spring comes, the fox's fur changes to brown or gray. It becomes the color of the ground.

The ptarmigan bird, or snow chicken, has white feathers in the winter. It, too, is hard to see in the snow. In the spring, the bird **molts**. This means that it sheds all of its feathers. The bird grows new feathers that are gray or brown and speckled. When the bird is very still, it looks like a rock.

17.   What is the passage mostly about?

   A.   how people change with the seasons

   B.   how seasons change

   C.   how animals change with the seasons

18.   What color is the arctic fox's fur in the winter?

   A.   brown   B.   white

   C.   black   D.   gray

19.   What happens to the ptarmigan bird in the spring?

   A.   It molts.   B.   It flies south.

   C.   Its feathers turn red.   D.   It hides near rocks.

20.   What does **molt** mean in the story?

   A.   to change colors   B.   to shed feathers

   C.   to hide from an enemy   D.   to run quickly

FITNESS FLASH: Do 10 sit-ups.

* See page ii.

PLACE
STICKER
HERE

Divide each set of objects into 3 equal groups. Then, divide to find each quotient.

1. $15 \div 3 =$ _____

2. $21 \div 3 =$ _____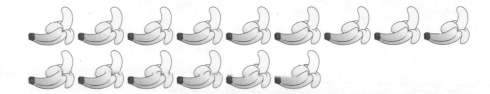

3. $9 \div 3 =$ _____

Circle and write the correct contraction to complete each sentence.
EXAMPLE:

___**They've**___ never played tennis.

They're   **They'll**   (**They've**)

4. _____ have a really fun time.

We're   **We'll**   **We've**

5. _____ work as hard as I can.

I'm   **I've**   **I'll**

6. _____ got to do it right the first time.

We've   **We'll**   **We're**

7. _____ going to see a movie tonight.

We'll   **We're**   **We've**

DAY 18

Read the story about Max and Julia. Write _M_ beside the phrases that describe Max, and _J_ beside the phrases that describe Julia. Write _B_ if the phrase describes both children.

Max and Julia

Max and Julia are twins. They have brown eyes and black hair. They are eight years old and go to school. Julia likes math, and Max likes to read. They both like to play outside. Julia likes to play basketball. Max likes to run and play tag. Julia likes to ride her bike while Max walks their dog, Rover.

8. _____ has brown eyes

9. _____ likes to run

10. _____ is a twin

11. _____ likes to play basketball

12. _____ likes to read

13. _____ likes math

14. _____ is eight

15. _____ has a pet

16. _____ likes to ride bikes

17. _____ has black hair

Write the letter of the correct definition next to each vocabulary word.

18. _____ desert

A.   a tall piece of land

19. _____ mountain

B.   a flowing body of water

20. _____ valley

C.   a body of water surrounded by land

21. _____ ocean

D.   low land between mountains or hills

22. _____ lake

E.   a place that is very dry

23. _____ river

F.   a body of water that surrounds continents

FACTOID: A group of frogs is called an _army_.

PLACE STICKER HERE

Important words in titles begin with capital letters. Look for the title in each sentence. Mark the letters that should be capitalized. Use this proofreading symbol: m.

1. Parker's favorite book is *A year of billy miller*.

2. Have you ever seen the movie *matilda*?

3. When Dad was little, he loved to watch *schoolhouse rock*.

4. Jaden knows all the words to his favorite song, "Don't worry, be happy."

5. Last weekend, we rented the movie *Against the wild*.

6. Grandma used to sing Cam to sleep by singing "walking after midnight."

To *abbreviate* a word means to shorten it. Draw a line to match each word to its abbreviation.

7.			8.		
	December	Dr.		Mister	Rd.
	Doctor	oz.		October	ft.
	Thursday	Dec.		foot	Mr.
	ounce	Jan.		Avenue	Ave.
	January	Thurs.		Road	Oct.

9.			10.		
	yard	Jr.		Saturday	Sr.
	March	Wed.		Senior	St.
	Junior	yd.		Monday	Mon.
	inch	in.		Fahrenheit	F
	Wednesday	Mar.		Street	Sat.

DAY 19

Abstract nouns name feelings, concepts, and ideas. Some examples are *hope*, *bravery*, and *pride*. Underline the abstract noun in each sentence.

11.   Mr. and Mrs. Ito were filled with pride when Jessica won the spelling bee.

12.   Mom always talks about the wonderful childhood she had with her sisters.

13.   My favorite thing about Jorge is his kindness.

14.   Cole could see the delight on Lea's face as she opened her gift.

15.   "I really appreciate your honesty," said Principal Jenkins.

16.   I can count on Lindsay to always tell me the truth.

Many doors lead to interesting places and things. Think of a door that could lead you to an interesting place. Describe the door and what is behind it. On a separate sheet of paper, draw a picture of your door.

_____

_____

_____

_____

_____

FITNESS FLASH: Do 10 squats.

* See page ii.

PLACE STICKER HERE

Quadrilaterals are four-sided shapes. Draw an example of each quadrilateral named below. In the last box, draw a different quadrilateral.

1. square	2. rectangle
3. rhombus	4. other

Estimate the mass of each item. Circle your answer.

5.

    A.   1 gram   B.   10 grams   C.   100 grams

6.

    A.   2 kilograms   B.   200 kilograms   C.   25 kilograms

7.

    A.   1 gram   B.   10 grams   C.   100 grams

8.

    A.   1 kilogram   B.   100 kilograms   C.   10 kilograms

CHARACTER CHECK: Brainstorm a list of positive, encouraging words and phrases. Refer to your list when you begin to feel discouraged with a task.

DAY 20

Read the poem. Then, answer the questions.

Two

Two living things, blowing in the wind.
One stands straight, the other bends.

One is a strong tree growing tall.
The other is grass ever so small.

Both are Mother Nature's gifts.
The tree you can climb. On the grass, you can sit.

Green is their color, brought on by the spring.
Grass or trees, they both make me sing!

9. What two things is the poem comparing?

    A. the grass and a tree

    B. a tree and a flower

    C. the wind and the rain

10. What does the line *Both are Mother Nature's gifts* mean?_____

_____

11. Read each description. Decide if the words describe the grass, a tree, or both.
    Write an X in each correct column.

Alike or Different?	Grass	Tree
living thing		
stands straight in the wind		
bends in the wind		
tall		
small		
can be climbed		
can be sat on		
green in color		

PLACE
STICKER
HERE

Paper Towel Preserver

Can you dunk a glass with a paper towel inside it into an aquarium filled with water and have the paper towel stay dry?

Materials:
- large, clear container or aquarium
- drinking glass (any size)
- dry paper towel
- water

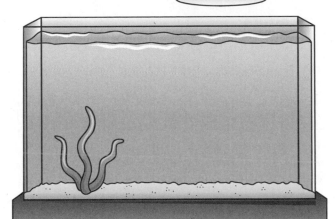

Procedure:
Have an adult help you fill the aquarium with water.

Gently stuff the paper towel into the bottom of the glass. Turn the glass upside down to make sure that the paper towel does not fall out.

Keep the glass upside down. Slowly lower it straight down into the container of water until

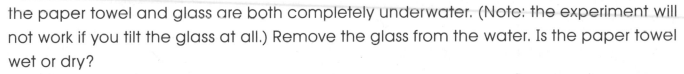

the paper towel and glass are both completely underwater. (Note: the experiment will not work if you tilt the glass at all.) Remove the glass from the water. Is the paper towel wet or dry?

What's This All About?
This experiment shows that air takes up space. As you lower the glass into the container of water, the air inside the glass displaces, or pushes away, the water in the container. Because the water is displaced, the paper towel stays dry.

More Fun Ideas to Try:
If you are having a hard time seeing how air takes up space, put your hands on your chest. Inhale, hold your breath, and then exhale. Did you feel how air takes up space in your lungs?

BONUS

Air Friction

Which would drop faster if it fell from a two-story building: a penny or a sheet of paper? Which would hit the ground first? How does air affect falling objects?

Materials:
- sheet of paper
- penny
- a few small, unbreakable objects

Procedure:

Hold the penny and the sheet of paper in front of you and higher than your head. Let them both fall at the same time. Repeat this activity two more times.

Now, crumple the paper into a tight ball. Hold the paper and the penny in front of you and higher than your head. Let them both fall at the same time. Repeat this activity two more times.

Repeat the experiment with two sheets of paper that are crumpled, one loosely and one tightly. Then, try different coins and other objects. Which object falls the fastest?

What's This All About?

Even though we cannot see air, it has force. By crumpling the paper, you reduced the amount of force the air was able to put on the paper. We call this force *friction*.

Sometimes, it is good to have a lot of air friction. For example, a person using a parachute would want friction. The friction created by the parachute would slow her descent to Earth. Sometimes, it is good to have less air friction, such as when a pilot wants to make an airplane fly fast.

More Fun Ideas to Try:

- Make a simple parachute that uses air friction to slow a falling object. Use different materials (paper, fabrics, plastic bags) to make the parachute.
- With an adult, find pictures of different types of cars on the Internet. Look at their designs. Which cars do you think would cause less air friction?

Think About It

- What is the purpose of the bold text below the title of the experiment?

Locate It!

A grid (set of lines on a map) and coordinates (the letters and numbers beside the grid) help you locate places on a map. To find the mall on the map, look at section B,2. Use the map grid and map key to fill in the blanks with the coordinates for each place.

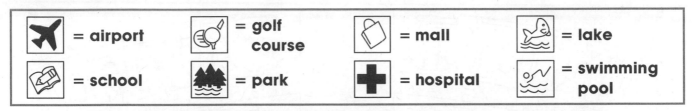

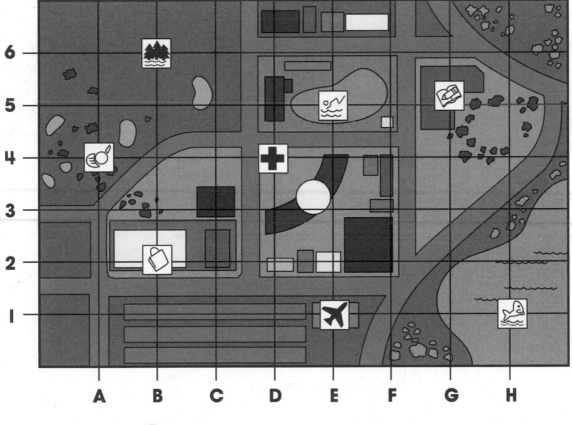

mall _____ **B, 2** _____   1. lake _____

2. school _____   3. park _____

4. airport _____   5. hospital _____

6. golf course _____   7. swimming pool _____

BONUS

Silver City Championship

Your favorite baseball team is in the championship game. Follow the steps to find out where your friends are sitting at the game.

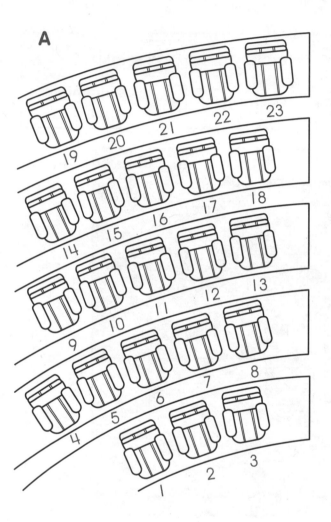

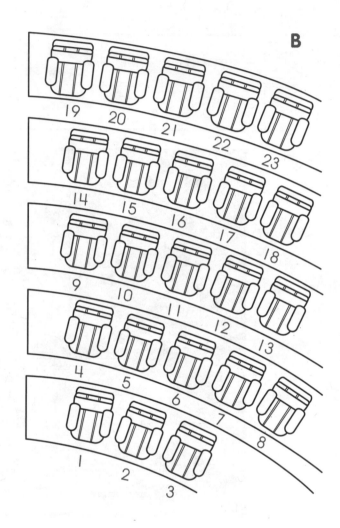

1. Greg is sitting in seat A, 11. Draw a red circle around Greg's seat.

2. Shauna is sitting in seat B, 9. Draw a blue square around Shauna's seat.

3. Craig is sitting in seat B, 5. Draw a green triangle around Craig's seat.

4. Phillip is sitting in seat A, 2. Color Phillip's seat orange.

5. Beth is sitting in seat A, 6. Color Beth's seat purple.

Continent Scramble

A *continent* is the largest landmass on Earth. There are seven continents in the world. List the seven continents by unscrambling each name. Then, look at the map. Write the letter of each continent next to its name.

1. _____ ACIFRA _____

2. _____ THORN MICAERA _____

3. _____ EPRUEO _____

4. _____ HOUTS RECIMAA _____

5. _____ SAAI _____

6. _____ CTARNATCAI _____

7. _____ STRLAIAUA _____

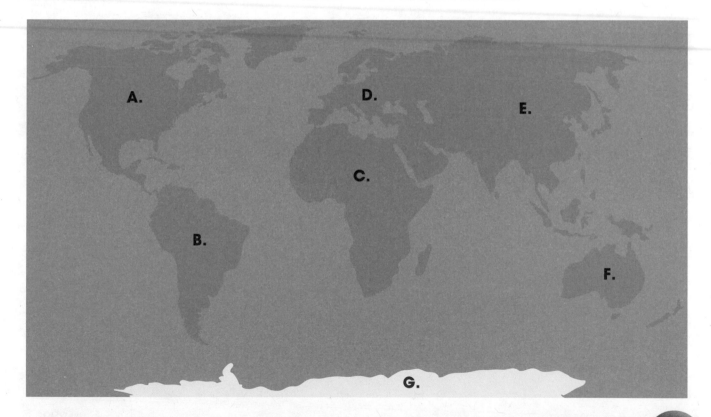

BONUS

Take It Outside!

Go outside with an adult. Take a notebook, a pencil, and a ruler that measures inches and centimeters. Find objects. Measure their lengths. Record each object's length in inches and centimeters. Compare the measurements. Which objects are the shortest, and which are longest?

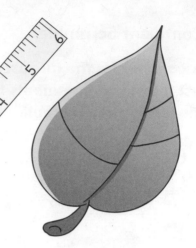

Play an outdoor observation game with a friend or family member. Find an object that is a three-dimensional geometric shape (sphere, cube, cylinder, cone, prism, or pyramid). Describe the shape to your friend. For example, to describe a beach ball, you would say, "I see a sphere." Take turns describing and identifying shapes.

Go outside with an adult. Take a pencil and a notebook. List some actions that have already happened. Examples include a house that has been built (built), a child who passed by (walked), a man getting out of a car (drove). When you are finished, look at the past-tense verbs on your list. Write a sentence with each verb.

* See page ii.

Monthly Goals

Think of three goals to set for yourself this month. For example, you may want to learn five new math facts each week. Write your goals on the lines and review them with an adult.

Place a sticker next to each goal that you complete. Feel proud that you have met your goals!

1. _____
   PLACE STICKER HERE

2. _____
   PLACE STICKER HERE

3. _____
   PLACE STICKER HERE

Word List

The following words are used in this section. They are good words for you to know. Read each word. Use a dictionary to look up each word that you do not know. Then, write two sentences. Use a word from the word list in each sentence.

channel   medal

election   pilot

festival   schedule

gigantic   sibling

mammal   vote

1. _____

_____

2. _____

_____

Introduction to Endurance

This section includes fitness and character development activities that focus on endurance. These activities are designed to get you moving and thinking about improving your physical fitness and your character.

Physical Endurance

What do playing tag, jumping rope, and riding your bike have in common? They are all great ways to build your endurance!

Having endurance means being able to do an activity for a long time before your body is tired. Your heart is stronger when you have endurance. Your muscles receive more oxygen.

Use the warm summer mornings and sunny days to go outside. Pick activities that you enjoy. Invite a family member on a walk or a bike ride. Play a game of basketball with friends. Leave the less active times for when it is dark, too hot, or raining.

Set an endurance goal this summer. For example, you might jump rope every day until you can jump for two minutes without stopping. Set new goals when you meet your old ones. Be proud of your endurance success!

Endurance and Character Development

Showing mental endurance means sticking with something. You can show mental endurance every day. Staying with a task when you might want to quit and trying your best until it is done are ways that you can show mental endurance.

Build your mental endurance this summer. Think of a time when you were frustrated or bored. Maybe you wanted to take swimming lessons. But, after a few early morning lessons, you were not having as much fun as you imagined. Think about some key points, such as how you asked all spring to take lessons. Be positive. Remind yourself that you have taken only a few lessons. You might get used to the early morning practices. Think of ways to make the lessons more enjoyable, such as sleeping a few extra minutes during the morning car ride. Quitting should be the last resort.

Build your mental endurance now. It will help prepare you for challenges that you may face later!

Tell one way in which the shapes in each pair are similar and different.

1.  _____

2. _____

3. _____

4. _____

Underline the verb that completes each sentence.

5. Benji and Kate (are, is) going on a fall scavenger hunt.

6. Benji (spot, spots) a pumpkin on a neighbor's porch.

7. Kate (sees, see) a scarecrow.

8. Leaves (dance, dances) along the sidewalk as a breeze blows.

9. The oak tree at the end of the street (drop, drops) acorns on the ground.

10. Busy squirrels (gather, gathers) the nuts.

11. The children (hears, hear) the sound of geese calling overhead.

DAY 1

Read the stories. Circle what happens next.

12. Jeff put his arms around the box. He could not lift it. He would need some help. The box was too heavy for him.

    Jeff will _____ .

    A. run outside and play   B. ask his dad for help

    C. sit on the box   D. send the box to his friend

13. The children were playing outside. It started to get dark. They saw a flash of light and heard a loud sound. The wind began to blow.

    "Let's go," shouted Hunter. "It's _____ ."

    A. time to eat   B. going to blow us away

    C. going to rain soon   D. time for bed

Use a conjunction from the box to complete each sentence. Do not use the same conjunction more than once.

and	although	while	but	or	because	until	whether

14. _____ Mom doesn't like coffee, she loves the way it smells.

15. Enzo took out the garbage, _____ Maria washed the dishes.

16. _____ the sun comes out or not, we will enjoy the party.

17. Mickey is almost a year old, _____ he is not walking yet.

18. Please don't open your gifts _____ your grandparents get here.

19. Samuel has to go to the doctor _____ he has an earache.

PLACE
STICKER
HERE

Michi is helping her dad build a chicken coop. Her dad asked her to measure the lengths of the boards in the garage. Draw an **X** on the line plot to show the measurement of each board.

Board A	$38\frac{1}{2}$ inches
Board B	$40\frac{3}{4}$ inches
Board C	$38\frac{1}{2}$ inches
Board D	$41\frac{1}{4}$ inches
Board E	$38\frac{1}{2}$ inches
Board F	$40\frac{3}{4}$ inches

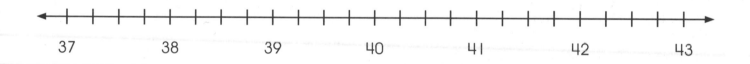

37   38   39   40   41   42   43

Add the ending shown to each base word to make a new word. Don't forget to change the spelling of the base word when the ending is added.

change *y* to *i*

1. try + s = _____

2. happy + ness _____

double the final consonant

3. sit + ing = _____

4. hop + ed = _____

drop the final *e*

5. smile + ed = _____

6. slide + ing = _____

change *ie* to *y* or *y* to *ie*

7. lie + ing = _____

8. puppy + s = _____

DAY 2

To find the *area* of a rectangle, multiply its length by its width. Solve each problem.

9. Tamika wants to buy a rug that is 5 feet wide by 7 feet long. What area will her rug cover?

_____ square feet

10. Jordan's backyard pool is 16 feet long by 10 feet wide. What is the area of his pool?

_____ square feet

11. Max got a tumbling mat for his birthday. It is 12 feet long by 6 feet wide. What is the area of the mat?

_____ square feet

12. Mr. O'Malley has to replace part of his garage roof. The damaged spot measures 5 feet wide by 3 feet long. What is its area?

_____ square feet

Imagine that you are collecting items for a time capsule that will be opened in 20 years. What things would you put in the capsule to tell about your life right now?

_____

_____

_____

_____

_____

PLACE STICKER HERE

Add or subtract to solve each problem.

1. 240
    + 125

2. 346
    + 231

3. 115
    + 460

4. 219
    + 674

5. 532
    + 164

6. 756
    − 110

7. 875
    − 241

8. 679
    − 336

9. 572
    − 320

10. 348
    − 123

11. 435
    + 281

12. 568
    + 272

13. 626
    + 193

14. 271
    + 378

15. 492
    + 247

Write _N_ if the verb is in the present tense (happening now). Write _P_ if the verb is in the past tense (already happened). Write _F_ if the verb is in the future tense (will happen in the future).

16. _____ We will eat later.

17. _____ I have a sandwich.

18. _____ Grant ate a pickle.

19. _____ We will go home soon.

20. _____ I love pickles!

21. _____ Mia is having a party.

22. _____ I swam with my friends.

23. _____ Ian cleaned his room.

FITNESS FLASH: Do 10 jumping jacks.

* See page ii.

DAY 3

Read the TV schedule. Then, answer the questions.

Time								
Channel		7:00	7:30	8:00	8:30	9:00	9:30	10:00	10:30
	2	Quiz Game Show	Jump Start		Summer the Dog			News	
	4	Lucky Guess	You Should Know	Wednesday Night at the Movies Friends Forever				News	
	5	Best Friends	Mary's Secret	Where They Are	Time to Hope	Tom's Talk Show		News	
	7	123 Oak Street	Lost Alone	One More Time	Sports			News	
	11	Your Health	Eating Right	Food News		Cooking With Kate		Home Decor	Shop Now
	24	Silly Rabbit	Clyde the Clown	Ball o' Fun	Slime and Rhyme	Cartoon Alley		Fun Times	Make Me Laugh

24. What does this schedule show?

   A. times and channels of TV shows

   B. times and channels of radio programs

   C. the number of people who like different shows

25. On which channels is the news on at 10:00?

   A. 2, 5, and 11   B. 3, 4, and 11   C. 2, 4, 5, and 7

26. What time does the show *Silly Rabbit* begin?

   A. 7:00   B. 7:30   C. 8:30

FACTOID: Camels have three sets of eyelids to protect their eyes from sand.

PLACE STICKER HERE

Follow the directions.

1. Draw lines to divide the square into 4 equal parts. Write numbers in the boxes to make a fraction that names one part.

2. Draw lines to divide the rectangle into 6 equal parts. Write numbers in the boxes to make a fraction that names one part.

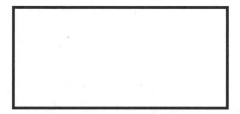

3. Draw lines to divide the circle into 3 equal parts. Write numbers in the boxes to make a fraction that names one part.

Change each declarative sentence into an interrogative sentence.
EXAMPLE:

The busy mail carrier is leaving. ____**Is the busy mail carrier leaving?**____

4. That man is Gary's father. _____

5. She can ride her new bike. _____

6. I will ride the black horse. _____

DAY 4

In a dictionary, guide words are at the top of each page. The guide word on the left tells the first word on the page. The guide word on the right tells the last word on the page. Circle the word that would be on the page with each set of guide words.

7. **patter — penguin**

   panda   pit   paw

8. **match — monkey**

   math   magic   motor

9. **bear — buffalo**

   bunny   bat   bison

10. **hammer — happy**

    hall   hand   hair

11. **rabbit — rack**

    race   racket   radio

Run for Fun and Endurance

Running is a great way to improve your endurance. Put on some comfortable running shoes and stretch for a few minutes. Whether you run in place, in the yard, or at the park, time how long you run. Repeat these runs a few times each week. After each run, record how long you ran. Try to increase the time slightly every week. By the end of the summer, you will be able to run longer and will have increased your endurance.

FITNESS FLASH: Jog in place for 30 seconds.

* See page ii.

PLACE STICKER HERE

Write a multiplication problem to find the area of each rectangle.

1.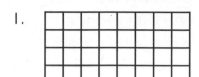

   Area = _____ × _____ = _____ square units

2.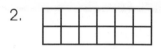

   Area = _____ × _____ = _____ square units

3.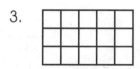

   Area = _____ × _____ = _____ square units

4.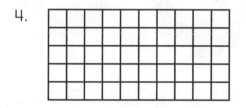

   Area = _____ × _____ = _____ square units

An exclamatory sentence shows strong emotions or feelings. Write _E_ for each exclamatory sentence. Write _D_ for each declarative sentence. Write _I_ for each interrogative sentence.

5. _____ What did they say?

6. _____ I am so happy for you!

7. _____ It's a boy!

8. _____ That is wonderful news!

9. _____ The card is green.

10. _____ Can I borrow a pencil?

Write each exclamatory sentence with a capital letter and an exclamation point (!).

11. watch out _____

12. i had a great day _____

DAY 5

Read the story. Then, complete the picture to match the story.

Margaret planted five flowers in pots. They grew fast. She put the flowers in a row. The white flower was in the middle. The purple flower was second. The orange flower was not first. The yellow flower was last. Where was the pink flower? Where does the orange flower go?

Write the missing comparative adjectives.

13.   fast   _____   _____

14.   _____   _____   tallest

15.   _____   colder   _____

16.   bright   _____   brightest

17.   _____   deeper   _____

18.   kind   _____   _____

PLACE STICKER HERE

Multiply to find each product. Then, draw a line to match each set to the correct multiplication problem.
EXAMPLE:

4 × 3 = __12__

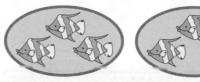

1.   3 × 3 = _____

2.   5 × 2 = _____

3.   3 × 2 = _____

4.   2 × 4 = _____

An imperative sentence gives a command. Write *IM* for each imperative sentence. Write *D* for each declarative sentence. Write *I* for each interrogative sentence. Write *E* for each exclamatory sentence.

5.   _____   Make a card for Mom.

6.   _____   Use markers.

7.   _____   She will love it!

8.   _____   Show your mom.

9.   _____   Tell her how you made it.

10.   _____   Cards are great gifts.

11.   _____   Has your dad seen it?

12.   _____   The card looks great!

Read the story. Then, answer the questions.

The Giant Cookie

My mother baked a giant cookie for me. I sat on my porch to eat it. But, before I could take a bite, my friend Ivy came by.

"Will you share your cookie with me?" Ivy asked. I broke my cookie into two pieces: one for me and one for Ivy. But, before we could each take a bite, Jermaine and Drew came by.

"Will you share your cookie with us?" they asked. Ivy and I each broke our cookie into two more pieces. Now, we had four pieces: one for me, one for Ivy, one for Jermaine, and one for Drew. But, before we could each take a bite, four more friends came by.

"Will you share your cookie with us?" they asked. Ivy, Jermaine, Drew, and I all broke our pieces in half. Now, we had enough to share between eight friends. I looked at my giant cookie. It was not a giant cookie anymore.

"Hey, does anyone know what is gigantic when there's one but small when there are eight?" I asked.

"No, what?" my friends asked.

"My cookie!" I laughed.

13. What happened to the cookie?

    A. It was shared between friends.   B. It was lost.

    C. It ran away.   D. It was dropped on the floor.

14. Number the events from the story in order.

    _____ Jermaine and Drew came by.

    _____ Mother baked a cookie.

    _____ Ivy came by.

    _____ Four friends came by.

FACTOID: Every ton of recycled paper saves about 24 trees.

PLACE STICKER HERE

Multiply to find each product.

1. 5 × 1 = _____

2. 5 × 5 = _____

3. 3 × 4 = _____

4. 1 × 0 = _____

5. 2 × 2 — _____

6, 4 × 5 = _____

7. 3 × 5 = _____

8. 1 × 1 = _____

9. 2 × 5 = _____

10. 7
    × 1

11. 4
    × 2

12. 2
    × 3

13. 3
    × 3

14. 4
    × 0

Write two exclamatory sentences and two declarative sentences. Use a word from the word bank in each sentence.

attention	calmly	famous	free	million
moment	rain	shiver	station	strange

15. _____

16. _____

17. _____

18. _____

CHARACTER CHECK: Brainstorm some obstacles you might encounter while trying to achieve your goals this summer. Write one way to overcome each obstacle.

DAY 7

Use the dictionary entry to answer the questions.

> **germ** \ˈjerm\ *n* **1.** disease-producing microbe **2.** a bud or seed

19. What part of speech is *germ*? _____

20. Which definition of *germ* deals with growing plants? _____

21. Would *germinate* come before or after *germ* in the dictionary? _____

22. Use *germ* in a sentence. _____

_____

Write a title for each list.

23. _____

    robin
    wren
    blue jay
    canary

24. _____

    paper
    glue
    scissors
    crayons

25. _____

    lion
    tiger
    bear
    elephant

26. _____

    milk
    tea
    water
    juice

FITNESS FLASH: Hop on your right foot for 30 seconds.

* See page ii.

PLACE STICKER HERE

Solve each problem.

1. Maddie has 3 vases with 4 flowers in each vase. How many total flowers does she have?

   _____ × _____ = _____ flowers

2. Mario has 4 packs of gum. There are 5 pieces in each pack. How many pieces of gum does he have?

   _____ × _____ = _____ pieces

3. Jawan has 3 glasses. He put 2 straws in each glass. How many straws did Jawan put in the glasses?

   _____ × _____ = _____ straws

4. We have 4 tables for the party. Each table needs 4 chairs. How many total chairs do we need?

   _____ × _____ = _____ chairs

Underline the pronoun that completes each sentence.

5. Caleb borrowed six books from the library, but he has lost one of (it, them).

6. At the fair, several kids lost (them, their) balloons.

7. Taj has three frogs as pets and loves (their, them) very much.

8. Liam remembered to brush (their, his) teeth before school.

9. The hurricane made landfall at 6:00, and (it, them) is headed this way!

10. Each of the girls gets an apple for (her, his) snack.

DAY 8

Read the paragraph. Then, answer the questions.

Megan's Day

Megan got up late today, so she missed the bus. Her mother had to walk Megan to school. She was tired and cranky when she got there. She promised herself that she would never sleep late again.

11. Why did Megan miss the bus? _____

12. Why did she have to walk? _____

_____

13. What advice do you have for Megan? _____

_____

Imagine that when you go to your mailbox one day, you find a treasure map with a letter addressed to you. Write a story about the letter and map. Who sent the letter? If you look for the treasure, do you find it? If you find it, what is it?

_____

_____

_____

_____

_____

_____

FACTOID: Deserts cover 25% of Earth's surface.

PLACE STICKER HERE

Divide each set of objects into 2 equal groups. Then, divide to find each quotient.

1.

6 ÷ 2 = _____

2.

4 ÷ 2 = _____

3.

10 ÷ 2 = _____

4.

8 ÷ 2 = _____

A *simple sentence* has one subject and one verb. A *compound sentence* is two simple sentences joined with a conjunction like *and*. A *complex sentence* is a simple sentence combined with a group of words called a *clause*.

Read each sentence below. On the line, write *S* if it is a simple sentence, *C* if it is a compound sentence, and *CX* if it is a complex sentence.

5. _____ The hummingbird drank from a flower, and then it flew away.

6. _____ Billy went to the park on Saturday.

7. _____ Because Lucia has a beautiful voice, she's going to take singing lessons this fall.

8. _____ Sarah plays basketball every day.

9. _____ Although the temperature dropped last night, the plants were okay.

10. _____ Ansel stopped at the library, but the book he ordered wasn't in yet.

115

DAY 9

Read the paragraph. Then, follow the directions.

Lauren's Summer

Lauren is very busy in the summer. She likes to sleep until eight o'clock. After she gets up, she helps her father work in the garden. Lauren reads and plays with her friends every day. She also likes to swim and play soccer with her brothers. Most of all, she likes to ride her bike.

11. Underline the topic sentence.

12. What time does Lauren get up? _____

13. How does Lauren help her father? _____

14. Write three other things that Lauren likes to do in the summer. _____

_____

Underline an adverb to complete each sentence.

15. Our puppy plays (more joyfully, joyfuller) with children than anyone else.

16. Joseph arrived (latest, most late) at the theater.

17. Please try to whisper (softer, more softly) while the baby sleeps.

18. Eli jumped (most farthest, farthest) of anyone in the competition.

19. The stars seem to shine (brightliest, most brightly) far from the city.

20. My sister completed the craft (carefullier, more carefully) than I did.

FITNESS FLASH: Hop on your left foot 10 times.

* See page ii.

PLACE STICKER HERE

DAY 10

Compare the fractions shown by the colored areas in each pair of circles. Use the greater than (>), less than (<), or equal to (=) symbols.

1.

2.

3.

4.

5.

6.

Capitalize the first, last, and all important words in a story or book title. Write each story title correctly.

EXAMPLE:

an exciting camping trip   <u>**An Exciting Camping Trip**</u>

7. my ride on a donkey _____

8. the day I missed school _____

9. fun, fabulous pets _____

10. a fire drill _____

11. my summer job _____

DAY 10

Numbers can be multiplied in different ways to get the same product. Write a product in each blank.

12. $(2 \times 3) \times 4 = 24$

   $6 \times 4 = $ _____

13. $3 \times 6 = 18$

   $6 \times 3 = $ _____

14. $(3 \times 4) + (3 \times 2) = 18$

   $3 \times (4 + 2) = $ _____

15. $15 \times 2 = 30$

   $2 \times 15 = $ _____

16. $(6 \times 2) \times 4 = 48$

   $12 \times 4 = $ _____

Similar words can have different shades of meaning. Write each word in the sentence where it makes the most sense.

17. **happy, overjoyed**

   Sonya was _____ to see her grandparents for the first time in nearly ten years.

   Lucas was _____ that he could sleep in on Saturday morning.

18. **cross, furious**

   Miguel felt _____ when he couldn't find his football helmet.

   Mrs. Hitch was _____ that the babysitter forgot to pick up the kids at school.

19. **gigantic, large**

   A _____ moth fluttered around the porch light.

   During the hurricane, several _____ waves nearly destroyed the village.

PLACE STICKER HERE

Divide to find each quotient.

1. $6\overline{)36}$ 2. $7\overline{)42}$ 3. $8\overline{)56}$ 4. $5\overline{)45}$

5. $3\overline{)21}$ 6. $9\overline{)63}$ 7. $4\overline{)36}$ 8. $6\overline{)54}$

Read the story. Circle each word that should have a capital letter. Then, answer the questions about the story.

Our Camping Trip

mom, dad, and i went camping last week. We went with Uncle seth and Aunt kay. We

had fun. Dad and uncle seth climbed on rocks. Aunt kay and I saw a chipmunk. We

all hiked on exciting trails. There was only one problem. mom, dad, and i did not bring

sweaters. Dad said that it would be warm in the desert. He was wrong. At night, it was

very cold. uncle Seth and aunt kay had sweaters. Mom, dad, and I stayed close to the

fire. Next time, we will bring warmer clothes.

9. What was Dad wrong about? _____

10. Who tells the story? _____

11. How do Mom, Dad, and the author solve their problem? _____

_____

DAY II

Read each sentence. Then, circle whether each sentence is reality or fantasy.

12. A beaver is a mammal that builds dams.
     reality   **fantasy**

13. The fairy lived inside a mushroom.
     reality   **fantasy**

14. People can build brick walls.
     reality   **fantasy**

15. The dog sang a song.
     reality   **fantasy**

Write a number in the star to complete each equation.

16. 8 × _____ = 56

17. _____ ÷ 9 = 2

18. 7 × 4 = _____

19. _____ × 10 = 90

20. 40 ÷ _____ = 8

21. 5 × _____ = 35

22. _____ × 3 = 21

23. 20 ÷ 4 = _____

24. _____ ÷ 6 = 6

25. 100 ÷ _____ = 10

FACTOID: Giraffes have very long tongues. They can lick their own eyes!

PLACE STICKER HERE

The fraction $\frac{3}{1}$ is the same as the whole number 3. Write numbers in the boxes to make a fraction that shows each whole number.

1. 5 ⬚/⬚

2. 11 ⬚/⬚

3. 24 ⬚/⬚

4. 9 ⬚/⬚

Answer the questions.

5. How many fourths make one whole? _____

6. How many eighths make one whole? _____

7. How many twelfths make one whole? _____

8. How many fifths make one whole? _____

Add commas and quotation marks where they are needed. Use this symbol to add a comma ⌒ and this symbol to add quotation marks ⌄ .

9. "Did you know that Reid lives in Dallas, Texas?

10. "Mr. Jarvis is my neighbor said Grandma.

11. Is Caleb's birthday in April?" asked Sasha.

12. "My mother and I shop at Smith's Market" I added.

13. What is your favorite month of the year? asked Rosie.

Read the passage. Then, answer the questions.

Amelia Earhart

Amelia Earhart was a famous airplane pilot. She was born in 1897. She saw her first airplane at the Iowa State Fair at age 10. Amelia Earhart started taking flying lessons in 1921. Then, she bought her first plane. She named the plane *Canary* because it was bright yellow.

In 1932, Amelia Earhart became the first woman to fly alone across the Atlantic Ocean. The U.S. Congress gave her a medal called the *Distinguished Flying Cross* after this accomplishment. Amelia Earhart set many new flying records. Also in 1932, she became the first woman to fly alone nonstop from one coast of the United States to another. In 1937, she decided to fly around the world. Her plane was lost over the Pacific Ocean. Amelia Earhart was never heard from again.

14. What is the main idea of this passage?

   A.   Amelia Earhart flew around the world.

   B.   Amelia Earhart was a famous pilot who set many flying records.

   C.   Amelia Earhart had a yellow airplane called *Canary*.

15. How does the author order or organize the information in this passage? _____

_____

16. Why did Earhart call her first airplane *Canary*? _____

17. Why did Earhart receive a medal? _____

_____

18. What happened to Earhart in 1937? _____

FITNESS FLASH: Do 10 jumping jacks.

* See page ii.

PLACE STICKER HERE

When you say, "It's raining cats and dogs," you don't really mean that animals are falling from the sky! You are using an expression, or an _idiom_. Write a sentence that uses each idiom below.

1. I'm all ears

   _____

2. green thumb

   _____

3. get the ball rolling

   _____

4. hit the hay

   _____

Unscramble and rewrite each sentence correctly. Add capital letters where they are needed. Write a period (.) or question mark (?) at the end of each sentence.

5. birds do live where _____

6. very my hard works sister _____

7. swim can like fish a she _____

8. green grass why is _____

9. water fish in live _____

10. park the go can when we to _____

11. the did go she to store why _____

12. is what name his _____

13. love to i play basketball _____

DAY 13

Read the story. Then, circle the letter of the best summary.

Water Fun

Larry loved to play in the water. Every time it rained, he would run outside to play in the puddles. His dog splashed in the water with him. Larry splashed water on anyone who came near. Soon, his friends would not play with him because he always got them wet. One day, a big truck went by and splashed water all over Larry. He got so wet that he decided not to splash people anymore.

14. A. Larry liked to play in puddles of water. He got wet. He did not splash anymore.

    B. Larry liked to play in puddles of water. He splashed water on people. One day, a truck splashed him. He stopped splashing others.

A Life Lesson

To *persevere* means to keep trying even when something is hard to do. Think of a time when you showed perseverance, such as when you learned to ride a bike. Try to remember how hard it was to learn but how exciting it was to reach your goal.

Take time to help a younger sibling or neighbor acquire a new skill. Explain the meaning of perseverance if he gets frustrated. Talk about how hard it was for you to learn a skill when you were younger. You can also share the goals you have now. Celebrate his success when he reaches his goal. Feel proud that you helped him persevere!

FACTOID: Peregrine falcons live on every continent except Antarctica.

PLACE
STICKER
HERE

Mark each fraction on the number line beside it.

1. $\frac{1}{2}$ 0 ——————— 1

    $\frac{3}{6}$ 0 ——————— 1

2. $\frac{2}{3}$ 0 ——————— 1

    $\frac{4}{6}$ 0 ——————— 1

3. $\frac{3}{4}$ 0 ——————— 1

    $\frac{6}{8}$ 0 ——————— 1

4. What do you notice about the fractions in each pair? _____

Add a simple sentence after each conjunction below to form a compound sentence.

EXAMPLE: Mr. Sanchez is a teacher, but

            Mr. Sanchez is a teacher, but he doesn't work at my school.

5. Dad is teaching Omar how to mow the lawn, but

_____

6. Hannah feeds the cats each morning, or

_____

7. It is supposed to snow on Tuesday, so

_____

8. Beatrix just joined the swim team, and

_____

DAY 14

Look at the index from a book about flowers. Then, write the page number where you would find the information on each flower.

9. tulip _____

10. pansy _____

11. daisy _____

12. rose _____

13. zinnia _____

14. lily _____

A	G	R
allium.......... 45	gardens.........2	rose 21
aster........... 62	gladiolus 7	S
B	I	stamen 6, 7
blossoms 13	iris 8	stigma....... 6, 7
buttercup 65	L	T
C	larkspur........47	thistle 27
cowslip 25	lily 42	tulip............. 26
D	M	W
daffodil........27	marigold 29	wisteria 20
dahlia 19	P	Z
daisy 15	pansy...........31	zinnia 60
	petals............6	

Think of something you know well. Do you love to play basketball or ice-skate? Do you enjoy baking or rock climbing? Are you crazy about dinosaurs or cats? Write a paragraph that shares information about a topic you know all about.

_____

_____

_____

_____

_____

_____

FITNESS FLASH: Jog in place for 30 seconds.

* See page ii.

PLACE STICKER HERE

Draw a line to match the shapes in each group that show the same fraction shaded.

1.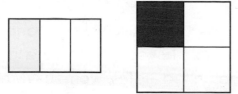

2.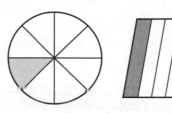

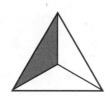   

Write the meaning of each underlined idiom.

3. Mrs. Wen <u>has her hands full</u> with the twins, who are two years old.

_____

4. After the storm, the flat tire, and Henry's tantrum, Mom was ready to <u>call it a day</u> and head home.

_____

5. I'm going to have to <u>hit the books</u> tonight if I want to be ready for the test.

_____

6. On accident, Olivia <u>spilled the beans</u> about the surprise party.

_____

7. Destiny <u>is a night owl</u>, but everyone else in her family goes to bed early.

_____

Read the passage. Then, answer the questions.

The Right to Vote

Voting in government elections is very important. In the United States and Canada, a person must be a citizen of the country and be at least 18 years old to vote in an election. Not everyone could vote in the past. In the United States, women were not allowed to vote until 1920. A law was passed in 1965 that gave adults of all races the right to vote. When a person votes, he or she helps decide who will serve in the government and what kinds of laws will be passed. Some people say that voting is the most important thing that people can do as citizens.

8.   What is the main idea of this passage?

   A.   A person must be at least 18 years old to vote in an election.

   B.   Not everyone can vote in the United States.

   C.   Voting is an important thing for people to be able to do.

9.   Who can vote in the United States and Canada? _____

   _____

10.   When were U.S. women first allowed to vote? _____

11.   What happened in the United States after a law was passed in 1965?

   _____

12.   Why is voting important? _____

   _____

CHARACTER CHECK: On another sheet of paper, explain why it is important to always try your best.

Color the objects to show each fraction.
EXAMPLE:

Color one-third.	1. Color two-fourths.	2. Color three-sixths.
$\frac{1}{3}$ 	$\frac{2}{4}$ 	$\frac{3}{6}$ 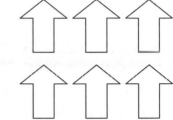
3. Color one-sixth.	4. Color one-fourth.	5. Color five-eighths.
$\frac{1}{6}$	$\frac{1}{4}$ 	$\frac{5}{8}$ 
6. Color three-fourths.	7. Color one-half.	8. Color two-thirds.
$\frac{3}{4}$	$\frac{1}{2}$ 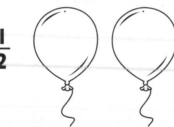	$\frac{2}{3}$ 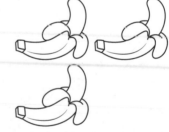

Add commas where they are needed in the paragraph.

Land Formations and Bodies of Water

The earth has many mountains, rivers, lakes oceans and continents. The Andes the

Rockies and the Urals are mountain ranges. The Amazon the Nile and the Hudson are

rivers. Lake Erie Lake Ontario and Lake Huron are three of the Great Lakes. The Pacific

the Atlantic and the Arctic are oceans. Europe, Asia and Africa are continents. New

Zealand Greenland and Iceland are islands.

DAY 16

Write the name of the person who is talking in each sentence.

9. Travis said, "Trent, you need to go to bed." _____

10. "Is this your book, Lamar?" asked Keisha. _____

11. Lamar replied, "No, Keisha, it is not my book." _____

12. "Will you take the dog for a walk, Mia?" asked Mrs. Travers. _____

13. "Would you please go to the store for me?" Sadaf asked. _____

Use the calendar to answer the questions.

August						
Sunday	**Monday**	**Tuesday**	**Wednesday**	**Thursday**	**Friday**	**Saturday**
		1	2	3	4	5
6	7	8	9	10	11	12
13	14	15	16	17	18	19
20	21	22	23	24	25	26
27	28	29	30	31		

14. What day of the week is August 18? _____

15. How many Wednesdays are in August? _____

16. What is the date of the last Saturday in August? _____

17. What day of the week will September 1 be? _____

FACTOID: A rhinoceros's horn isn't really a horn. It's made of tightly pressed hair.

PLACE STICKER HERE

Do you wish you had a later bedtime? Write a letter to your parent(s) or guardian explaining your opinion. Include good reasons to support your opinion.

_____

_____

_____

_____

_____

_____

_____

Rewrite each sentence correctly. Add capital letters, periods, and question marks where they are needed.

1. bobby has a dog named shadow

   _____

2. do bluebirds eat insects

   _____

3. can i borrow your video game

   _____

4. my name is nikki _____

DAY 17

An *analogy* compares two pairs of items based on a similar relationship between the items. Write the correct word from the word bank to complete each analogy.

| cat | ground | window | ~~water~~ | trees | cow |

EXAMPLE:

Car is to road as boat is to _____ **water** _____ .

5. Bird is to sky as worm is to _____ .

6. City is to buildings as forest is to _____ .

7. Knob is to door as pane is to _____ .

8. Cub is to bear as calf is to _____ .

9. Quack is to duck as meow is to _____ .

Fitness Festival

Invite a few friends or family members to a fitness festival. Set up three exercise stations for endurance activities. These could include jumping rope, running in place, hopping on one foot, or doing jumping jacks. Take turns rotating through each station. Rest after each exercise and sip some water. Complete each station twice. After everyone has completed the fitness activities, celebrate together with a healthy snack.

 FITNESS FLASH: Hop on your left foot 10 times.

* See page ii.

PLACE STICKER HERE

The bar graph shows concession stand sales at a baseball game. Use the bar graph to answer the questions.

1. Which two items had the fewest sales?

   _____

2. Which item had the most sales?

   _____

3. How many more nachos were sold

   than hot dogs?_____

4. How many more chips were sold

   than pretzels? _____

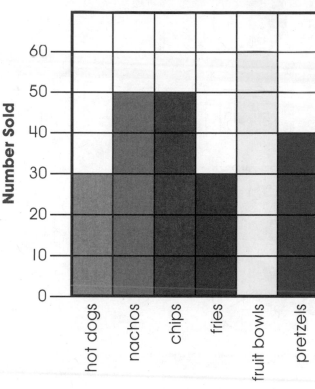

Concession Stand Sales

Snacks

Write three sentences. Use a word from the word bank in each sentence. Use capital letters, periods, question marks, and exclamation points where they are needed.

adult	during	finish	interested
job	prepare	summer	work

5. _____

6. _____

7. _____

DAY 18

Draw a line between fractions that are equivalent, or equal.

$\frac{1}{2}$

$\frac{4}{6}$

$\frac{4}{4}$

$\frac{1}{3}$

$\frac{3}{9}$

$\frac{2}{4}$

$\frac{2}{3}$

$\frac{1}{1}$

Imagine that one morning you woke up, looked outside, and spotted a dinosaur walking down your street. What would happen next? Write a story telling about your experience.

_____

_____

_____

_____

_____

FACTOID: Giant bamboo plants can grow nine inches per day!

PLACE STICKER HERE

The line graph shows precipitation changes during a year in Chicago, Illinois. Use the line graph to answer the questions.

Precipitation Changes

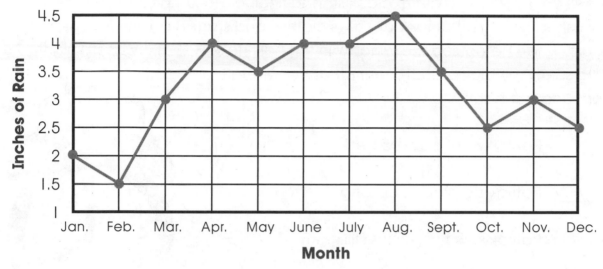

1. Which three months received the same amount of rain?

_____

2. What was the most rainfall received in one month? _____

3. Which month received the least amount of precipitation?_____

Use a dictionary to look up the word *consequence*. Why should you think about consequences?

_____

_____

_____

_____

DAY 19

Read the story. Number the events in the order that they happened.

The Alarm Clock

Patrick was sleeping when his alarm clock started ringing. He jumped up, made his bed, and washed his face. Patrick put on his clothes and started going downstairs to eat breakfast. When he passed the window in the hall, he saw that it was still night. "Oh, no," he said, "my alarm clock went off at the wrong time!" Patrick went back to his bedroom and got back into bed.

4. _____ Patrick went back to bed.

5. _____ Patrick's alarm clock rang.

6. _____ Patrick saw that it was still night.

7. _____ Patrick made his bed and washed his face.

8. _____ Patrick started going downstairs to eat breakfast.

What would you do if you woke up and you had become your mom or dad? What would your day be like?

_____

_____

_____

_____

_____

FITNESS FLASH: Hop on your right foot for 30 seconds.

* See page ii.

PLACE STICKER HERE

Study the pictograph. Then, answer the questions.

Number of Flowers Picked

 = 2 flowers

Allie	🌼 🌼 🌼	Beth	🌼 🌼 🌼 🌼 🌼 🌼
Sue	🌼 🌼 🌼 🌼 🌼	Lori	🌼 🌼 🌼 🌼 🌼
Danny	🌼 🌼	Jamal	🌼 🌼 🌼 🌼

1. How many flowers does 🌼 stand for? _____

2. How many total flowers did Sue and Allie pick? _____

3. Who picked the most flowers? _____

4. Which children picked the same number of flowers? _____

5. Who picked the fewest flowers? _____

Write the part of speech for each underlined word. Write your answer above the word.

Vegetables

Do you like <u>vegetables</u>? I like some vegetables. I do not like others. I like snow peas.

<u>They</u> taste best fresh from the garden. They are green and sweet. I like fresh, <u>crunchy</u>

carrots, too. I pick them from the garden. I <u>love</u> corn on the cob. I pull off the husks.

Mom <u>boils</u> the corn. I eat the <u>yellow</u> corn from one end to the other.

DAY 20

Read the story. Then, answer the questions.

Ready for the Play-Off

Austin was too excited about the baseball play-off game to think about the model volcano he and Pablo were building in science class.

"Do you want to tear the paper into strips or dip them in paste and put them on?" Pablo asked.

"Home run!" said Austin.

Pablo looked puzzled. Austin's face burned with embarrassment. "I'm sorry. I was thinking about the game."

Pablo laughed. "Oh!" he said. "Well, that explains it. Do you think we'll win?"

"My big brother says that Ms. Lee's class hasn't won a play-off game in at least five years. Maybe we'll be the first," Austin said.

Austin saw Ms. Lee walking toward them. He picked up a piece of newspaper and tore it into strips. Pablo understood. He dipped a strip into the paste and smoothed it onto the side of the model volcano.

"You boys should start cleaning up now," Ms. Lee said. "We don't want to be late."

Austin and Pablo carried their model to the science table, put the lid on the paste container, recycled the extra newspaper, and cleaned their work area. They were back in their seats and ready to go in five minutes.

6.   Who is the main character in the story?

   A.   Austin's brother   B.   Austin   C.   Ms. Lee

7.   What does the main character want to do? _____

   _____

8.   Where does the story take place?

   A.   in a classroom   B.   in a gym   C.   on the baseball field

9.   In the fourth paragraph, what does *Austin's face burned with embarrassment*

   mean?_____

   _____

PLACE STICKER HERE

An Oily Separation

How can a mixture of oil and water be separated?

Materials:

- 16-ounce clear drinking glass
- spoon
- eyedropper
- 6.75 ounces (200 mL) of water
- 6.75 ounces (200 mL) of vegetable oil
- clear glass measuring cup

Procedure:

Pour the water into the drinking glass. Add the vegetable oil to the water. Stir the water and oil with the spoon and observe. Then, let the water and oil sit for 10–15 minutes.

Use the eyedropper to pull the oil from the top of the water and place it into the measuring cup. Record the amount of oil collected. Then, subtract that amount from the amount of oil that was first added to the drinking glass. Record your results. Then, try the experiment two more times. Record your data in the table.

Trial	Initial Volume of Oil	Volume of Oil Collected	Difference
1			
2			
3			

1. What happens when you stir the water and the oil? _____

    _____

2. What happens when you stop stirring the water and the oil? _____

    _____

What's This All About?

Sometimes, liquids separate into layers. Oil and water separate into layers. Water is heavier than oil, so it sinks to the bottom of a container.

Think About It

- What is an eyedropper? Why do you need to use one for this experiment?
- What causes and effects can be seen in this experiment?

BONUS

Disappearing Act

Water can disappear by evaporating. Sometimes, water leaves things behind when it evaporates.

Materials:

- masking tape
- 2 pie tins
- drinking glass
- 1 tablespoon of salt
- measuring cup
- pencil
- water
- spoon

Procedure:

Use the masking tape and a pencil to label the outside of the pie tins. Label the first pie tin *salt water* and the second pie tin *tap water*.

Use the measuring cup to pour 4 ounces (11.8 cL) of warm water into a drinking glass. Add one tablespoon of salt to the water. Use the spoon to stir the water until the salt dissolves. Add salt until no more will dissolve. This is called a *saturated solution*. Pour the saturated solution into the pie tin labeled *salt water*.

Use the measuring cup to pour 4 ounces (11.8 cL) of tap water into the pie tin labeled *tap water*. Put the pie tins side-by-side in a safe place. Record your observations each day until the water in both pie tins has evaporated.

What's This All About?

This activity uses salt water as the basis for crystal formation. The water evaporates from the pan. Salt, a mineral, stays in the pan.

More Fun Ideas to Try:

- Change the amount of salt in the water. Find out if it affects how quickly the water evaporates.
- With an adult, change the liquid you use. Try vinegar, lemonade, etc. Use the same amount of salt and change the amount of liquid.

Land Features

Look at the map. Write the letter of each landform next to its name.

1. _____ lake
2. _____ valley
3. _____ river
4. _____ peninsula
5. _____ volcano
6. _____ island
7. _____ mountain
8. _____ ocean
9. _____ savanna

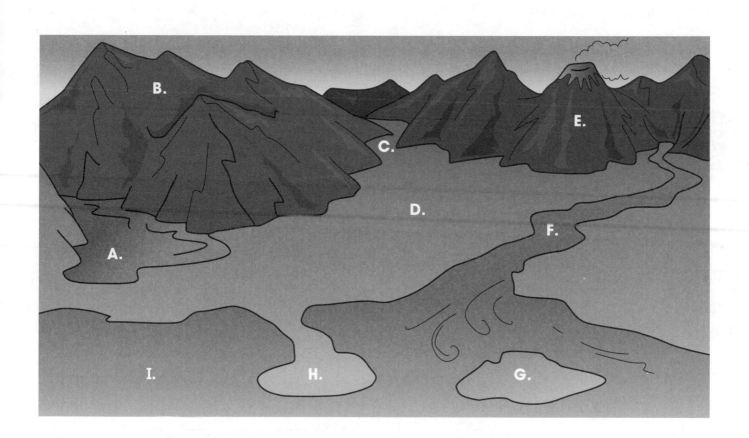

BONUS

Countries and Cities

Political maps show landmasses divided into regions such as countries and cities. Study a map of North America in an atlas or on the Internet. Then, draw a line to connect each city to its country. You will use each country more than once.

City

1. Mexico City
2. Toronto
3. Washington, D.C.
4. Montreal
5. Chicago
6. Acapulco
7. Boston
8. Guadalajara
9. Phoenix
10. New York City

Country

Mexico

Canada

United States of America

Choose one country from the list above, or pick a country you are interested in studying. Use an encyclopedia or the Internet to find information about this country. Then, write three facts about the country on the lines.

_____

_____

_____

_____

_____

_____

Democratic Governments

Read the passage. Then, answer the questions.

There are many types of government. One type of government is a democratic government. A democratic government gives its citizens the power to make decisions.

The United States has a democratic government. In the United States, citizens elect a president. The president is the head of the government. The citizens also elect people to Congress. Congress is the branch of government that makes laws. Great Britain also has a democratic government. The prime minister is the head of the government in Great Britain. The prime minister also helps make laws.

1. There are many types of _____ .

2. A _____ government gives its citizens the power to make decisions.

3. In the United States, the _____ elect a president.

4. In the United States, the _____ is the head of the government.

5. Citizens of the United States also elect people to _____ .

6. Congress is the branch of government that makes _____ .

7. In Great Britain, the _____ helps make the laws.

8. What other kinds of government are there? Go to the library or go online with an adult to learn about a country that does not have a democratic government. How is that country's government similar to and different from yours?

_____

_____

_____

BONUS

Take It Outside!

Summer is full of spectacular scenes and inspiration. One of the most amazing sights of summer is the bright and beautiful flowers. Look for an interesting plant that catches your attention or a pretty flower in a garden or field. Instead of picking the plant or flower, keep it alive and pass on its beauty to others. Take a photograph of your plant or draw a picture of it. Turn your flower artwork into a "thinking of you" card and send it to someone you are not able to see this summer.

Math is everywhere—even outside! Watch for word problem opportunities when you are outdoors. For example, if you see 12 seagulls flying in the air, 3 more splashing in a puddle, and 16 sitting on the pier, write these facts on a piece of paper and turn them into a word problem. Solve the problem. Then, challenge your family and friends with your outdoor math problem.

With an adult, find a few different flowers outside. Look at each flower and identify its parts (petal, sepal, carpel, stamen, and stigma). Compare each flower's parts with the others' parts to find the similarities and differences.

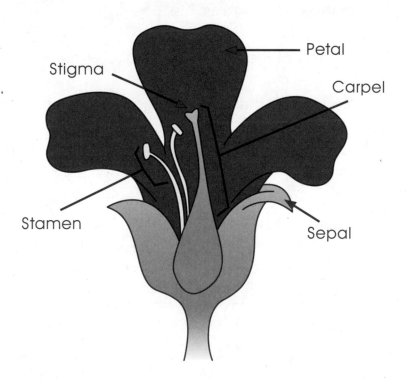

* See page ii.

Section I

Day 1/Page 3: 1. 45; 2. 58; 3. 881; 4. 30; 5. 362; 6. 912; From left to right and top to bottom: zero, twenty, thirty, forty, sixty, eighty; 7. Students should draw a triangle.; 8. Students should draw a hexagon.; 9. Students should draw a circle or an oval.; 10. 700, 800, 900, 1,000, Rule: Add 100.; 11. 50, 60, 70, 80, 90, 100, Rule: Add 10.; 12. 25, 30, 35, 40, 45, 50, Rule: Add 5.; 13. Avery wanted to bike to the park, but he got a flat tire.; 14. Mr. Greene coaches our soccer team, and I think he does a great job.; 15. The fireworks lit up the night sky, so everyone cheered.; 16. Tanesha is moving to Illinois, but her family hasn't found a house yet.

Day 2/Page 5: 1. 63¢; 2. 52¢; 3. 62¢; 4. 51¢; 5. 6; 6. 3; 7. 8; 8. 7; 9. pencil, sundae, helmet, dragon; 10. blossom, rabbit, spider, tiger; 11. carrot, puppy, candy, seven; 12. wonder, summer, cricket, marry; 13. candle, pencil, muffin, circus; 14. peanut, dollar, mitten, window

Day 3/Page 7: 1. 346; 2. 527; 3. 831; 4. 730; 5. 292; 6. 214; 7. 428; 8. 400; 9. 479; 10. 872; 11. 680; 12. 722; 13. 399; 14. 600; 15. 735; 16. Students should color 1 of 4 parts.; 17. Students should color 2 of 3 parts.; 18. Students should color 4 of 4 parts.; 19. Students should color 1 of 3 parts.; 20. Students should color 1 of 2 parts.; 21. Students should color 3 of 4 parts.; 22. C; 23. to explain how insects and arachnids can be helpful; 24. They move pollen from flower to flower.; 25. They eat insects that chew on plants.; 26. Crops are plants that farmers grow. The phrase "fruits and vegetables" is a clue.

Day 4/Page 9: 1. <; 2. >; 3. >; 4. <; 5. <; 6. >; 7. >; 8. <; 9. <; 10. <; 11. >; 12. <; 13. 14, even; 14. 9, odd; 15. 18, even; 16. 62; 17. 207; 18. 124; 19. 214; 20. 195; 21. 84; 22. 168; 23. 125; 24. 139; 25. L; 26. S; 27. L; 28. S; 29. S; 30. L; 31. S; 32. L; 33. L; 34. S; 35. L

Day 5/Page 11: 1. 2 hundreds; 2. 1 ten; 3. 3 tens; 4. 3 hundreds; 5. 0 tens; 6. Students should divide the circle into 4 equal parts, fourth.; 7. Students should divide the triangle into 2 equal parts, half.; 8. Students should divide the rectangle into 3 equal parts, third.; 9. 25; 10. 122; 11. 60; 12. 435; 13. 142; 14. 99; 15. short; 16. long; 17. short; 18. short; 19. long; 20. short; 21. long; 22. short; 23. short; 24. long; 25. short; 26. long; 27. long; 28. short; 29. long; 30. long

Day 6/Page 13: 1. 629, 682, 636, 660; 2. 879, 429, 609, 509, 889, 469, 209; 3. 231, 38, 639, 530, 333, 32; 4. 354, 151, 555, 250, 658, 50, 255; 5. 423, 484, 432, 422; 6. 327, 147, 607, 447, 997, 207; 7. Austin, Texas; 8. Valentine's Day; 9. France; 10. Papa Pete's; 11. Nashville, Tennessee; 12. Crunch Os; 13. St. Patrick's Day; 14. A; 15. travel quickly and easily from one coast of the United States to the other; 16. eastern and western parts of the country; 17. a golden nail; 18. Answers will vary, but may include that railroads helped carry people and goods and connected the two coasts of the United States.

Day 7/Page 15: Book measurements will vary, but each should be rounded to the nearest whole inch and recorded on the line plot.; Holidays: Memorial Day, Thanksgiving, Kwanzaa; Products: Sparkling Bubbles body wash, Clarabelle's pies, Orchard

Plus frozen fruit; Places: Russia, Appalachian Mountains, Mexico City, St. Louis; 1. 500 + 20 + 8; 2. 100 + 30; 3. 600 + 80 + 9; 4. 400 + 20 + 1; 5. 700 + 8; 6. 500 + 60 + 7; 9. 900 + 60 + 3; 10. 800 + 6; Students' writing will vary.

Day 8/Page 17: 1. 3 inches, 7 centimeters; 2. 4 inches, 9 centimeters; 3. 2 inches, 6 centimeters; 4. Students should circle *loudly* and underline *barked*.; 5. Students should circle *everywhere* and underline *looked*.; 6. Students should circle *faster* and underline *swims*.; 7. Students should circle *slowly* and underline *walked*.; 8. Students should circle *early* and underline *awoke*.; 9. Students should circle *outside* and underline *play*.; 10. re-, D; 11. un-, B; 12. mis-, A; 13. un-, E; 14. *mis-*, C; 15. 2, 2; 16. 4, 2; 17. 1, 1; 18. 3, 3; 19. 2, 1; 20. 1, 1; 21. 2, 2; 22. 2, 2; 23. 3, 3; 24. 2, 2; 25. 2, 1; 26. 2, 2; 27. 2, 1; 28. 3, 2; 29. 5, 3; 30. 2, 2

Day 9/Page 19: 1. 6 + 5 = 11, 5 + 6 = 11, 11 − 6 = 5, 11 − 5 = 6; 2. 4 + 5 = 9, 5 + 4 = 9, 9 − 5 = 4, 9 − 4 = 5; 3. 7 + 5 = 12, 5 + 7 = 12, 12 − 7 = 5, 12 − 5 = 7; 4. Students should divide the rectangle into 3 rows and 5 columns, 15.; 5. Students should divide the rectangle into 4 rows and 6 columns, 24.; 6. Students should divide the rectangle into 2 rows and 7 columns, 14.; 7. -ness; 8. -less; 9. -ness; 10. -ness; 11. -ness; Students should write the following words under the fly: dry, eye, sky.; Students should write the following words under the baby: city, happy, story.

Day 10/Page 21: 1. +; 2. −; 3. −; 4. =; 5. +; 6. −; 7. −; 8. −; 9. =; 10. −; 11. =; 12. +; 13. +; 14. +; 15. −; 16. 3 + 3 + 3 + 3 + 3 = 15; 17. 8 + 8 = 16; 18. 7 + 7 + 7 = 21; 19. rain/drop; 20. light/house; 21. door/bell; 22. barn/

yard; 23. bed/room; 24. snow/ flakes

Day 11/Page 23: 1. 63 marbles; 2. 24 apples; 3. 63 minutes; 4. 67 puppies; 5. gulped; 6. shattered; 7. gobble; 8. furious; 9. tapped; 10. A, B; 11. B, A; 12. B, A; Students should circle the following words: zoo, hoop, soon, pool, scoop, cool, stool, food, moon, moose, goose, school, tool, boot, spoon.; Students should draw Xs on the following words: book, wool, cook, hood, took, brook, foot, wood, crook, stood.

Day 12/Page 25: 1. A; 2. I; 3. B; 4. D; 5. E; 6. J; 7. K; 8. F; 9. G; 10. H; 11. men; 12. teeth; 13. leaves; 14. geese; 15. knives; 16. mice; 17. feet; Students should write the following words under *animals*: fox, elephant, bear, deer.; Students should write the following words under *tools*: saw, pliers, hammer, screwdriver.; Students should write the following words under *clothing*: shirt, pants, socks, hat.; 18. colony; 19. fleet; 20. swarm; 21. bouquet; 22. school

Day 13/Page 27: 1. 40; 2. 20; 3. Cats and No Pets; 4. 60; 5. Taylor's; 6. computer's; 7. Digby's; 8. Ana's; 9. Mom's; 10. C; 11. as long as it takes to sing the alphabet; 12. washes away germs that make you sick; 13. B; 14. You could pass sickness to a friend and spread the germs to your eyes and mouth.

Day 14/Page 29: 1. 758; 2. 599; 3. 851; 4. 320; 5. 516; 6. 466; 7. 904; 8. 171; 9. 1,000; 10. I; 11. 95, Students should mark the number line beginning on 60 and ending on 95.; 12. 36, Students should mark the number line beginning on 22 and ending on 36.; 13. 70, Students should mark the number line

beginning on 100 and ending on 70.; 14. 65, Students should mark the number line beginning on 85 and ending on 65. 15. I planted seeds.; 16. Luke started his car.; 17. I put on my socks.; 18. We built a snowman.; 19. I put toothpaste on my toothbrush.; 20. I climbed into bed.; Students' writing will vary.

Day 15/Page 31: 1. =, <, >; 2. <, =, =; 3. =, <, <; 4. =, <, =; 5. >, <, =; 6. dis<u>obey</u> = not obey; 7. re<u>appear</u> = appear again; 8. un<u>lucky</u> = not lucky; 9. dis<u>honest</u> = not honest; 10. pre<u>order</u> = order before; 11. un<u>safe</u> = not safe; 12. re<u>write</u> = write again; 13. pre<u>cook</u> = cook before; 14. C

Day 16/Page 33: 1. 34 flowers; 2. 28 laps; 3. 32 cars; 4. 43 toys; 5. 34 centimeters; 6. 6 inches; 7. 153 meters; 8. 39 pounds; 9. A; 10. oceans, lakes, and streams; 11. Drops of water rise into the air.; 12. when the air cools; 13. They produce rain, snow, sleet, or hail.; 14. The author's purpose is to provide information about the water cycle.

Day 17/Page 35: 1. 42; 2. 24; 3. 89; 4. 14; 5. 78; 6. 12; 7. 13; 8. 0; 9. 35; 10. 48; 11. 86; 12. 97; 13. 6; 14. 14; 15. 11; 16. myself; 17. themselves; 18. himself; 19. itself; 20. herself; 21. yourself; 22. B; 23. A; 24. phone; 25. elephants; 26. alphabet; 27. amphibian

Day 18/Page 37: 1. 449; 2. 977; 3. 589; 4. 338; 5. 472; 6. 757; 7. 813; 8. 747; 9. 804; 10. 288; 11. 871; 12. 895; 13. 407; 14. 800; 15. 682; 16. unsure, not sure; 17. unhappy, not happy; 18. unable, not able; 19. rewrite, write again; 20. retell, tell again; 21. reprint, print again; Students' writing will vary.;

22. ; 23. ; 24. ; 25. , 5:50; 26.

Day 19/Page 39: 1. 598; 2. 100; 3. 582; 4. 813; 5. 107; 6. 478; 7. 422; 8. 760; 9. 72; 10. 56; 11. C; 12. B; 13. jump into bed too; 14. the boy; 15. everywhere the boy goes; 16. Yes, it has a steady beat because the syllables of the words form a pattern.; 17. w; 18. b; 19. k; 20. k; 21. k, gh; 22. b

Day 20/Page 41: 1. 389; 2. 855; 3. 363; 4. 388; 5. 106; 6. 59; 7. 301; 8. 203; 9. 605; 10. 778; 11. 993; 12. 790; 13. 999; 14. 900; 15. 840; Students should write the following words under *present*: blow, find, fly, know, laugh, wear.; Students should write the following words under *past*: blew, flew, found, knew, laughed, wore.; 16. F; 17. R; 18. R; 19. F; 20. F; 21. R; 22. F; 23. R; 24. F; 25. F ; Students' writing will vary.

Bonus Page 44: 1. the marble that traveled through water; 2. Answers will vary.

Bonus Page 45: Yellow Sands

Bonus Page 46:

Bonus Page 47: 1. Shady Oaks Street; 2. Clear Creek Road; 3. Main Street; 4. Windy Way; 5. Walnut Street; 6. Shady Oaks Street and Park Street

Section II

Day 1/Page 51: 1. 111; 2. 115; 3. 47; 4. 114; 5. 111; 6. 82; 7. 120; 8. 112; 9. 132; 10. 83; 11. 50; 12. 41; 13. 124; 14. 58; 15. 95; 16. slept; 17. held; 18. made; 19. won; 20. left; 21. fell; 22. bought; 23. Chloe's baseball mitt; 24. Jasper's soccer ball; 25. Trinity's goggles; 26. Grandpa's golf clubs; 27. Cassidy's ballet shoes; 28. Ian's tennis racquet; 29. incorrect; 30. incorrect; 31. correct; 32. incorrect; 33. correct

Day 2/Page 53: 1. 49; 2. 45; 3. 8; 4. 56; 5. 59; 6. 17; 7. 39; 8. 75; 9. 15; 10. 46; 11. 19; 12. made; 13. took; 14. bought; 15. saw; 16. went; 17. flew; 18. A; 19. C; 20. play outside, go swimming

Day 3/Page 55: 1. 451; 2. 734; 3. 839; 4. 448; 5. 682; 6. 526; 7. 225; 8. 381; 9. 628; 10. 992; 11. am; 12. is; 13. are; 14. am; 15. are; 16. is; 17. are; 18. 6 × 3 = 18; 19. 3 × 10 = 30; 20. 7 × 4 = 28

Day 4/Page 57: 1. 15; 2. 28; 3. 5; 4. 6; 5. noun; 6. adverb; 7. adjective; 8. verb; 9. pronoun; 10. verb; 11. Students should mark $\frac{3}{4}$ on the number line.; 12. Students should mark $\frac{5}{8}$ on the number line.; 13.

Students should mark $\frac{1}{3}$ on the number line.; 14. Students should mark 1 on the number line.

81 Riverwood Rd.
Charlotte , NC 28870
;
1425 Newtown Terrace #12
Providence , RI 02906
;
132 West Billingsley Lane
Taos , NM 87571
;
21896 Langston Blvd.
San Diego , CA 92119

Day 5/Page 59: 1. √; 2. X; 3. √; 4. X; 5. √; 6. X; 7. X; 8. √; 9. X; 10. √; 11. √; 12. √; 13. X; 14. √; 15. X; 16. have; 17. has; 18. has; 19. has; 20. have; 21. have; 22. has; 23. has; 24. B; 25. F; 26. T; 27. T; 28. F; 29. Students' paragraphs will vary.

Day 6/Page 61: 1. 1:25; 2. 11:07; 3. 3:56; 4. 2:38; 5. 10:40; 6. 7:22; 7. one who gardens; 8. not honest; 9. process of adding; 10. not fiction; 11. not healthy; 12. state of being ill; 13. one who collects; 14. use again; 15. Students should circle *reason*. Possible answer: *reasoning*; 16. Students should circle *interest*. Possible answer: *interests*; 17. Students should circle *behave*. Possible answer: *behaved*; 18. Students should circle *believe*. Possible answer: *believable*; 19. Students should circle *cycle*. Possible answer: *unicycle*; 20. Students should circle *phone*. Possible answer: *phonograph*; Students' writing will vary.

Day 7/Page 63:

1. ; 2. ;

3. ; 4. ;

5. ; 6. ;

7. raked, raking; 8. jumped, jumping; 9. hugged, hugging; 10. cooked, cooking; 11. skated, skating; 12. wrapped, wrapping; 13. sneezed, sneezing; 14. popped, popping; 15. talked, talking; 16. smiled, smiling; 17. C; 18. E; 19. D; 20. B; 21. A; 22. 24 in.; 23. 15 in.; 24. 20 cm; 25. 43 in.; 26. 195 mm; 27. 40 cm

Day 8/Page 65: 1. 7:50; 2. 4:45; 3. 6:50; 4. 11:30; 5. went; 6. gone; 7. went; 8. gone; 9. went; 10. more than 900; 11. insects, fruit, and nectar; 12. 16 inches (40 cm) in length; 13. The main idea of the first paragraph is that bats help people in many ways.; 14. The author provides the following evidence to support the main idea: bats eat insects, and bats pollinate and spread the seeds of many plants. 15. mosquitoes, mayflies, and moths

Day 9/Page 67:

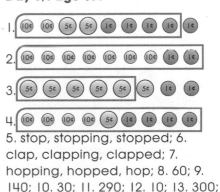

5. stop, stopping, stopped; 6. clap, clapping, clapped; 7. hopping, hopped, hop; 8. 60; 9. 140; 10. 30; 11. 290; 12. 10; 13. 300;

14. 600; 15. 200; 16. 700; 17. 800

Day 10/Page 69: Students should draw 4 loaves for January, 4 loaves for February, 6 loaves for March, 8 loaves for April, 8 $\frac{1}{2}$ loaves for May, and 9 $\frac{1}{2}$ loaves for June.; Yesterday, we **learned** about colors in art. We **made** a color wheel. We found out that there **are** three basic colors. They **are** called *primary colors*. Red, yellow, and blue are primary colors. Primary colors mix to make other colors. Red and yellow **make** orange. Yellow and blue make green. Blue and red make purple. Orange, green, and purple **are** secondary colors.; 1. B; 2. A; 3. B; 4. A; 5. A; 6. 180; 7. 350; 8. 360; 9. 240; 10. 240; 11. 270; 12. 480; 13. 80; 14. 60; 15. 70

Day 11/Page 71:

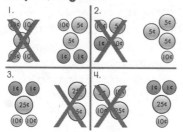

5. equal; 6. tiny; 7. low; 8. rainy; 9. B; 10. Africa, Antarctica, Asia, Australia, Europe, North America, South America; 11. millions of years ago; 12. jungle; 13. They were once one piece of land.

Day 12/Page 73: 1.–5. Answers will vary.; 6. soft; 7. steep; 8. screechy; 9. hot, wet; 10. 540, 500, 500 + 40 + 2; 11. 310, 300, 300 + 10 + 1; 12. 900, 900, 800 + 90 + 8; 13. 430, 400, 400 + 20 + 6; 14. 660, 700, 600 + 50 + 7; 15. 100, 100, 100 + 2; Students' writing will vary.

Day 13/Page 75: 1. 6 × 2 = 12, 12 + 4 = 16; 2. 8 × 6 = 48, 55 – 48 = 7; 3. 27 ÷ 9 = 3, 12 × 3 = 36; 4. blue, purple; 5. little, green; 6. colorful, soft; 7. dark, gray; 8. new, brown; 9.

2; 10. 1; 11. 4; 12. 3

Day 14/Page 77: 1. 1 + 3 + 1 = 5 inches; 2. 3 + 2 + 1 = 6 inches; 3. 1 + 4 + 2 = 7 inches; Students' writing will vary.; 4. A; 5. 8–11 hours each night; 6. You might have trouble paying attention to your teacher.; 7. read a book; 8. C

Day 15/Page 79: 1. 7 cm; 2. 8 cm; 3. 9 cm; 4. 3 cm; 5. 5 cm; 6. 4 cm; 7.–11. Answers will vary.; 12. C; 13. B; Students' writing will vary.

Day 16/Page 81: 1. A; 2. B; 3. A; 4. B; 5. B; 6. I am; 7. you will; 8. would not; 9. we have; 10. we would; 11. you are; 12. she is; 13. is not; 14. I will; 15. page 4; 16. Chapter 3; 17. page 26; 18. All About Ants; 19. electric; 20. train; 21. keep; 22. truck; 23. play

Day 17/Page 83: 1. C; 2. B; 3. B; 4. A; 5. she is; 6. he is; 7. are not; 8. you have; 9. I have; 10. I would; 11. it is; 12. have not; 13. she will; 14. should not; 15. we will; 16. we are; 17. C; 18. B; 19. A; 20. B

Day 18/Page 85: 1. 5; 2. 7; 3. 3; 4. We'll; 5. I'll; 6. We've; 7. We're; 8. B; 9. M; 10. B; 11. J; 12. M; 13. J; 14. B; 15. B; 16. J; 17. B; 18. E; 19. A; 20. D; 21. F; 22. C; 23. B

Day 19/Page 87: 1. Year, Billy, Miller; 2. Matilda; 3. Schoolhouse Rock; 4. Worry, Be, Happy; 5. Wild; 6. Walking, After, Midnight; 7. December—Dec., Doctor—Dr., Thursday—Thurs., ounce—oz., January—Jan.; 8. Mister—Mr., October—Oct., foot—ft., Avenue—Ave., Road—Rd.; 9. yard—yd., March—Mar., Junior—Jr., inch—in., Wednesday—Wed.; 10. Saturday—Sat., Senior—Sr., Monday—Mon., Fahrenheit—F, Street—St.; 11. pride; 12. childhood; 13. kindness; 14. delight; 15. honesty; 16. truth; Students' writing

will vary.

Day 20/Page 89: 1. Students should draw a square.; 2. Students should draw a rectangle.; 3. Students should draw a rhombus (diamond).; 4. Students should draw any shape with four sides that does not fit the definition of a square, rectangle, or rhombus.; 5. A; 6. C; 7. B; 8. C; 9. A; 10. It means that both trees and grass are good things for humans that come from nature.; 11.

Alike or Different?	Grass	Tree
living thing	X	X
stands straight in the wind		X
bends in the wind	X	
tall		X
small	X	
can be climbed		X
can be sat on	X	
green in color	X	X

Bonus Page 93: 1. H,1; 2. G,5; 3. B,6; 4. E,1; 5. D,4; 6. A,4; 7. E,5

Bonus Page 94:

Bonus Page 95: 1. C, Africa; 2. A, North America; 3. D, Europe; 4. B, South America; 5. E, Asia; 6. G, Antarctica; 7. F, Australia

Section III

Day 1/Page 99: 1. Possible answers: The shapes are similar because they both have four sides and four corners. The shapes are different because the square's sides are all equal and the rectangle's sides are not equal.; 2. Possible answers: The shapes are similar because they are both two-dimensional. The shapes are different because the triangle has three sides and the square has four sides.; 3. Possible answers: The shapes are similar because they both have no sides. The shapes are different because the circle is round and the oval is not round.; 4. Possible answers: The shapes are similar because they both have four equal sides. The shapes are different because the square has straight corners and the rhombus does not.; 5. are; 6. spots; 7. sees; 8. dance; 9. drops; 10. gather; 11. hear; 12. B; 13. C; Answers may vary. Possible answers: 14. Although; 15. and; 16. Whether; 17. but; 18. until; 19. because

Day 2/Page 101:

1. tries; 2. happiness; 3. sitting; 4. hopped; 5. smiled; 6. sliding; 7. lying; 8. puppies; 9. 35 square feet; 10. 160 square feet; 11. 72 square feet; 12. 15 square feet; Students' writing will vary.

Day 3/Page 103: 1. 365; 2. 577; 3. 575; 4. 893; 5. 696; 6. 646; 7. 634; 8. 343; 9. 252; 10. 225; 11. 716; 12. 840; 13. 819; 14. 649; 15. 739; 16. F; 17. N; 18. P; 19. F; 20. N; 21. N; 22. P; 23. P; 24. A; 25. C; 26. A

Day 4/Page 105: 1. Students should divide the square into 4 equal parts, $\frac{1}{4}$.; 2. Students should divide the rectangle into 6 equal parts, $\frac{1}{6}$.; 3. Students should divide the circle into 3 equal parts, $\frac{1}{3}$.; 4. Is that man Gary's father?; 5. Can she ride her new bike?; 6. Will I ride the black horse?; 7. paw; 8. math; 9. bison; 10. hand; 11. race

Day 5/Page 107: 1. 8 × 4 = 32

square units; 2. 6 × 2 = 12 square units; 3. 5 × 3 = 15 square units; 4. 10 × 5 = 50 square units; 5. I; 6. E; 7. E; 8. E; 9. D; 10. I; 11. Watch out!; 12. I had a great day!; From left to right: pink, purple, white, orange, yellow; 13. faster, fastest; 14. tall, taller; 15. cold, coldest; 16. brighter; 17. deep, deepest 18. kinder, kindest

Day 6/Page 109:

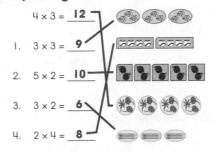

5. IM; 6. IM; 7. E; 8. IM; 9. IM; 10. D; 11. I; 12. E; 13. A; 14. 3, 1, 2, 4

Day 7/Page 111: 1. 5; 2. 25; 3. 12; 4. 0; 5. 4; 6. 20; 7. 15; 8. 1; 9. 10; 10. 7; 11. 8; 12. 6; 13. 9; 14. 0; 15–18. Answers will vary.; 19. noun; 20. 2. a bud or a seed; 21. after; 22. Answers will vary.; 23. birds; 24. school supplies; 25. animals; 26. drinks

Day 8/Page 113: 1. 3 × 4 = 12 flowers; 2. 4 × 5 = 20 pieces; 3. 3 × 2 = 6 straws; 4. 4 × 4 = 16 chairs; 5. them; 6. their; 7. them; 8. his; 9. it; 10. her; 11. She got up late today.; 12. She missed the bus.; 13. Answers will vary.; Students' writing will vary.

Day 9/Page 115:

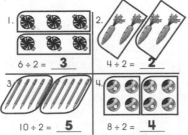

5. C; 6. S; 7. CX; 8. S; 9. CX; 10. C; 11. *Lauren is very busy in the summer.*; 12. eight o'clock; 13. She helps him work in the garden.; 14. Answers will vary but may include: swimming, playing soccer, reading, playing with friends, and riding her bike.; 15. more joyfully; 16. latest; 17. more softly; 18. farthest; 19. most brightly; 20. more carefully

Day 10/Page 117: 1. >; 2. <; 3. >; 4. >; 5. >; 6. <; 7. My Ride on a Donkey; 8. The Day I Missed School; 9. Fun, Fabulous Pets; 10. A Fire Drill; 11. My Summer Job; 12. 24; 13. 18; 14. 18; 15. 30; 16. 48; 17. overjoyed, happy; 18. cross, furious; 19. large, gigantic

Day 11/Page 119: 1. 6; 2. 6; 3. 7; 4. 9; 5. 7; 6. 7; 7. 9; 8. 9; **Mom**, **Dad**, and **I** went camping last week. We went with Uncle **Seth** and Aunt **Kay**. We had fun. Dad and **Uncle Seth** climbed on rocks. Aunt **Kay** and I saw a chipmunk. We all hiked on exciting trails. There was only one problem. **Mom**, **Dad**, and **I** did not bring sweaters. Dad said that it would be warm in the desert. He was wrong. At night, it was very cold. **Uncle** Seth and **Aunt Kay** had sweaters. Mom, **Dad**, and I stayed close to the fire. Next time, we will bring warmer clothes.; 9. Dad thought that the author would be warm in the desert.; 10. The story is told from a child's point of view.; 11. They stay close to the fire.; 12. reality; 13. fantasy; 14. reality; 15. fantasy; 16. 7; 17. 18; 18. 28; 19. 9; 20. 5; 21. 7; 22. 7; 23. 5; 24. 36; 25. 10

Day 12/Page 121: 1. $\frac{5}{1}$; 2. $\frac{11}{1}$; 3. $\frac{24}{1}$; 4. $\frac{9}{1}$; 5. 4; 6. 8; 7. 12; 8. 5; 9. "Did you know that Reid lives in Dallas, Texas?"; 10. "Mr. Jarvis is my neighbor," said Grandma.;

11. "Is Caleb's birthday in April?" asked Sasha.; 12. "My mother and I shop at Smith's Market," I added.; 13. "What is your favorite month of the year?" asked Rosie.; 14. B; 15. The author gives the information in time order.; 16. It was bright yellow.; 17. She was the first woman to fly alone across the Atlantic Ocean.; 18. She decided to fly around the world. Her plane was lost over the Pacific Ocean.

Day 13/Page 123: Answers will vary. Possible answers: 1. Go ahead and tell me, I'm all ears.; 2. You can tell from Mom's garden that she has a green thumb.; 3. Hurry up! It's time to get the ball rolling.; 4. I know it's only 8:00, but I think it's time for me to hit the hay.; 5. Where do birds live?; 6. My sister works very hard.; 7. She can swim like a fish./Can she swim like a fish?; 8. Why is grass green?; 9. Fish live in water.; 10. When can we go to the park?; 11. Why did she go to the store?; 12. What is his name?; 13. I love to play basketball.; 14. B

Day 14/Page 125: 1. Students should mark $\frac{1}{2}$ and $\frac{3}{6}$ on the number lines.; 2. Students should mark $\frac{2}{3}$ and $\frac{4}{6}$ on the number lines.; 3. Students should mark $\frac{3}{4}$ and $\frac{6}{8}$ on the number lines.; 4. Each pair of fractions shown is equivalent.; Possible answers: 5. Dad is teaching Omar how to mow the lawn, but Nabil is too young.; 6. Hannah feeds the cats each morning, or they meow until she wakes up.; 7. It is supposed to snow on Tuesday, so I'm hoping school is canceled.; 8. Beatrix just joined the swim team, and her first swim meet is in July.; 9. 26; 10. 31; 11. 15; 12. 21; 13. 60; 14. 42; Students' writing will vary.

Day 15/Page 127:

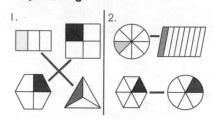

3. is very busy; 4. quit, be done; 5. study, read; 6. told the news/secret; 7. likes to stay up late; 8. C; 9. all citizens over the age of 18; 10. 1920; 11. Adults of all races were given the right to vote.; 12. People can help decide who serves in the government and what kinds of laws are passed.

Day 16/Page 129:

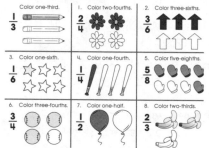

The earth has many mountains, rivers, lakes, oceans, and continents. The Andes, the Rockies, and the Urals are mountain ranges. The Amazon, the Nile, and the Hudson are rivers. Lake Erie, Lake Ontario, and Lake Huron are three of the Great Lakes. The Pacific, the Atlantic, and the Arctic are oceans. Europe, Asia, and Africa are continents. New Zealand, Greenland, and Iceland are islands.; 9. Travis; 10. Keisha; 11. Lamar; 12. Mrs. Travers; 13. Sadaf; 14. Friday; 15. 5; 16. 26; 17. Friday

Day 17/Page 131: Students' writing will vary.; 1. Bobby has a dog named Shadow.; 2. Do bluebirds eat insects?; 3. Can I borrow your video game?; 4. My name is Nikki.;

5. ground; 6. trees; 7. window; 8. cow; 9. cat

Day 18/Page 133: 1. hot dogs and fries; 2. fruit bowls; 3. 20; 4. 10; 5.–7. Answers will vary.; Students should draw a line between $\frac{1}{2}$ and $\frac{2}{4}$, $\frac{4}{6}$ and $\frac{2}{3}$, $\frac{4}{4}$ and 1, $\frac{1}{3}$ and $\frac{3}{9}$.; Students' writing will vary.

Day 19/Page 135: 1. April, June, July; 2. 4.5 inches; 3. February; Students' writing will vary.; 4. 5; 5. 1; 6. 4; 7. 2; 8. 3; Students' writing will vary.

Day 20/Page 137: 1. 2; 2. 16; 3. Beth; 4. Sue and Lori; 5. Danny; noun; pronoun; adjective; verb; verb; adjective; 6. B; 7. win the play-off game; 8. A; 9. It means that Austin's face turned red because he was embarrassed.

Bonus Page 139: 1. It looks like they mix together.; 2. They separate.

Bonus Page 141: 1. A; 2. C; 3. F; 4. H; 5. E; 6. G; 7. B; 8. I; 9. D

Bonus Page 142: 1. Mexico; 2. Canada; 3. United States of America; 4. Canada; 5. United States of America; 6. Mexico; 7. United States of America; 8. Mexico; 9. United States of America; 10. United States of America; Facts will vary.

Bonus Page 143: 1. government; 2. democratic; 3. citizens; 4. president; 5. Congress; 6. laws; 7. prime minister; 8. Students' writing will vary.

joked	rolled	pre–
im–	dis–	–ed
–ing	–ly	possible

like	agree	test
© Carson-Dellosa	© Carson-Dellosa	© Carson-Dellosa
made	wish	cook
© Carson-Dellosa	© Carson-Dellosa	© Carson-Dellosa
friend	climb	slow
© Carson-Dellosa	© Carson-Dellosa	© Carson-Dellosa

3 × 3	6 × 2	1 × 5
© Carson-Dellosa	© Carson-Dellosa	© Carson-Dellosa
5 × 2	7 × 3	2 × 3
© Carson-Dellosa	© Carson-Dellosa	© Carson-Dellosa
9 × 2	4 × 2	8 × 8
© Carson-Dellosa	© Carson-Dellosa	© Carson-Dellosa

$\begin{array}{r} 1 \\ \times\ 5 \\ \hline 5 \end{array}$	$\begin{array}{r} 6 \\ \times\ 2 \\ \hline 12 \end{array}$	$\begin{array}{r} 3 \\ \times\ 3 \\ \hline 9 \end{array}$
© Carson-Dellosa	© Carson-Dellosa	© Carson-Dellosa
$\begin{array}{r} 2 \\ \times\ 3 \\ \hline 6 \end{array}$	$\begin{array}{r} 7 \\ \times\ 3 \\ \hline 21 \end{array}$	$\begin{array}{r} 5 \\ \times\ 2 \\ \hline 10 \end{array}$
© Carson-Dellosa	© Carson-Dellosa	© Carson-Dellosa
$\begin{array}{r} 8 \\ \times\ 8 \\ \hline 64 \end{array}$	$\begin{array}{r} 4 \\ \times\ 2 \\ \hline 8 \end{array}$	$\begin{array}{r} 9 \\ \times\ 2 \\ \hline 18 \end{array}$
© Carson-Dellosa	© Carson-Dellosa	© Carson-Dellosa

2 × 2	8 × 2	3 × 9
© Carson-Dellosa	© Carson-Dellosa	© Carson-Dellosa
9 × 9	5 × 5	7 × 2
© Carson-Dellosa	© Carson-Dellosa	© Carson-Dellosa
1 × 8	8 × 5	4 × 6
© Carson-Dellosa	© Carson-Dellosa	© Carson-Dellosa

3 × 9 27	8 × 2 16	2 × 2 4
7 × 2 14	5 × 5 25	9 × 9 81
4 × 6 24	8 × 5 40	1 × 8 8

6 × 6	1 × 4	7 × 5
© Carson-Dellosa	© Carson-Dellosa	© Carson-Dellosa
4 × 4	6 × 4	2 × 6
© Carson-Dellosa	© Carson-Dellosa	© Carson-Dellosa
5 × 7	9 × 5	3 × 4
© Carson-Dellosa	© Carson-Dellosa	© Carson-Dellosa

$$\begin{array}{r} 7 \\ \times\ 5 \\ \hline 35 \end{array}$$

$$\begin{array}{r} 1 \\ \times\ 4 \\ \hline 4 \end{array}$$

$$\begin{array}{r} 6 \\ \times\ 6 \\ \hline 36 \end{array}$$

© Carson-Dellosa

© Carson-Dellosa

© Carson-Dellosa

$$\begin{array}{r} 2 \\ \times\ 6 \\ \hline 12 \end{array}$$

$$\begin{array}{r} 6 \\ \times\ 4 \\ \hline 24 \end{array}$$

$$\begin{array}{r} 4 \\ \times\ 4 \\ \hline 16 \end{array}$$

© Carson-Dellosa

© Carson-Dellosa

© Carson-Dellosa

$$\begin{array}{r} 3 \\ \times\ 4 \\ \hline 12 \end{array}$$

$$\begin{array}{r} 9 \\ \times\ 5 \\ \hline 45 \end{array}$$

$$\begin{array}{r} 5 \\ \times\ 7 \\ \hline 35 \end{array}$$

© Carson-Dellosa

© Carson-Dellosa

© Carson-Dellosa

$2\overline{)6}$

$1\overline{)2}$

$2\overline{)8}$

$1\overline{)3}$

$3\overline{)3}$

$3\overline{)9}$

$4\overline{)4}$

$4\overline{)12}$

$5\overline{)10}$

$2\overline{)8}^{\,4}$

$1\overline{)2}^{\,2}$

$2\overline{)6}^{\,3}$

$3\overline{)9}^{\,3}$

$3\overline{)3}^{\,1}$

$1\overline{)3}^{\,3}$

$5\overline{)10}^{\,2}$

$4\overline{)12}^{\,3}$

$4\overline{)4}^{\,1}$

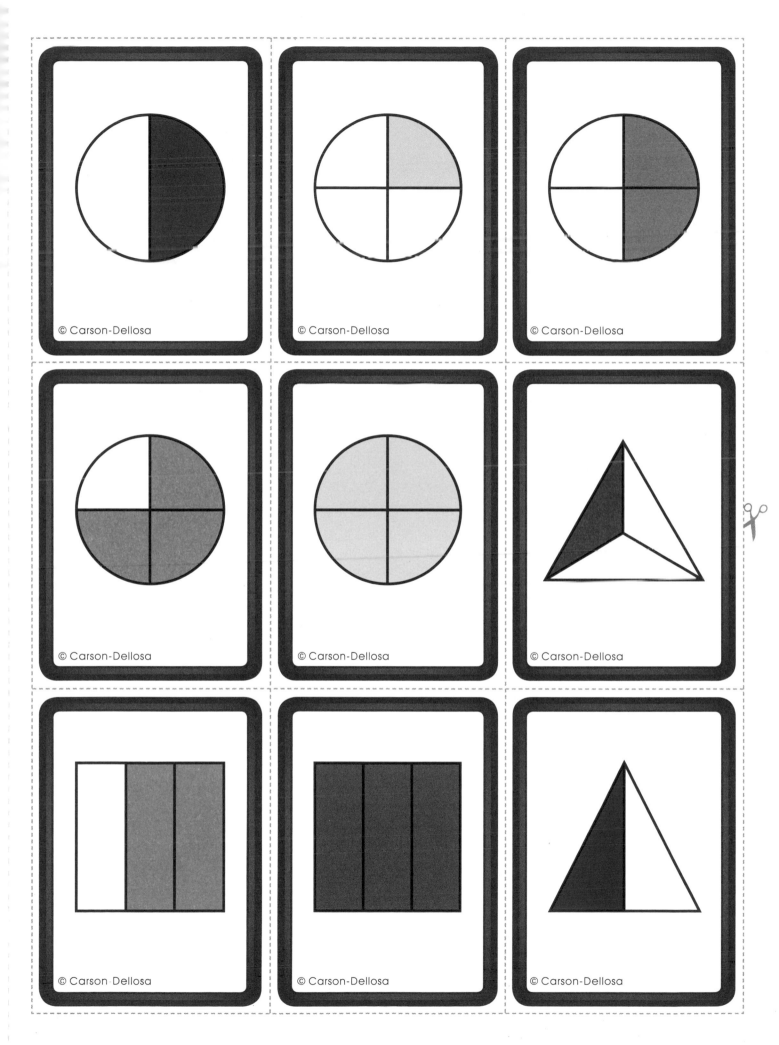

$\dfrac{2}{4} = \dfrac{1}{2}$

$\dfrac{1}{4}$

$\dfrac{1}{2}$

© Carson-Dellosa

© Carson-Dellosa

© Carson-Dellosa

$\dfrac{1}{3}$

$\dfrac{4}{4} = 1$

$\dfrac{3}{4}$

© Carson-Dellosa

© Carson-Dellosa

© Carson-Dellosa

$\dfrac{1}{2}$

$\dfrac{3}{3} = 1$

$\dfrac{2}{3}$

© Carson-Dellosa

© Carson-Dellosa

© Carson-Dellosa

Summer Bridge Activities®

Congratulations!

This certifies that

_____
Name

has completed **Summer Bridge Activities.**

_____
Parent's Signature